DEFINING MOMENTS
THE DREAM OF AMERICA:
IMMIGRATION
1870-1920

DEFINING MOMENTS
THE DREAM OF AMERICA:
IMMIGRATION
1870-1920

Kevin Hillstrom

Omnigraphics

P.O. Box 31-1640
Detroit, MI 48231

Omnigraphics, Inc.

Kevin Hillstrom, *Series Editor*
Cherie D. Abbey, *Managing Editor*

Peter E. Ruffner, *Publisher*
Matthew P. Barbour, *Senior Vice President*

Elizabeth Collins, *Research and Permissions Coordinator*
Kevin M. Hayes, *Operations Manager*

Allison A. Beckett and Mary Butler, *Research Staff*
Cherry Stockdale, *Permissions Assistant*
Shirley Amore, Martha Johns, and Kirk Kauffman, *Administrative Staff*

Copyright © 2009 Omnigraphics, Inc.
ISBN 978-0-7808-1070-9

Library of Congress Cataloging-in-Publication Data

Hillstrom, Kevin, 1963-
 The dream of America : immigration 1870-1920 / by Kevin Hillstrom.
  p. cm. -- (Defining moments)
 Includes bibliographical references and index.
 Summary: "Provides a detailed account of U.S. immigration from 1870 to 1920. Explores the forces that drove emigrants to the U.S.; shows what they experienced when they arrived; and reviews the history of U.S. immigration through the present. Includes a narrative overview, biographies, primary sources, chronology, glossary, bibliography, and index"--Provided by publisher.
 ISBN 978-0-7808-1070-9 (hardcover : alk. paper) 1. United States--Emigration and immigration--History. I. Title.
 JV6453.H56 2009
 304.8'7309034--dc22
                                                                        2008049921

The information in this publication was compiled from the sources cited and from other sources considered reliable. Additional copyright information can be found on the photograph credits page of this book and accompanying every reprinted source. While every possible effort has been made to ensure reliability, the publisher will not assume liability for damages caused by inaccuracies in the data, and makes no warranty, express or implied, on the accuracy of the information contained herein.

This book is printed on acid-free paper meeting the ANSI Z39.48 Standard. The infinity symbol that appears above indicates that the paper in this book meets that standard.

Printed in the United States

TABLE OF CONTENTS

PRIMARY SOURCES

PREFACE

Throughout the course of America's existence, its people, culture, and institutions have been periodically challenged—and in many cases transformed—by profound historical events. Some of these momentous events, such as women's suffrage, the civil rights movement, and U.S. involvement in World War II, invigorated the nation and strengthened American confidence and capabilities. Others, such as the McCarthy era, the Vietnam War, and Watergate, have prompted troubled assessments and heated debates about the country's core beliefs and character.

Some of these defining moments in American history were years or even decades in the making. The Harlem Renaissance and the New Deal, for example, unfurled over the span of several years, while the American labor movement and the Cold War evolved over the course of decades. Other defining moments, such as the Cuban missile crisis and the terrorist attacks of September 11, 2001, transpired over a matter of days or weeks.

But although significant differences exist among these events in terms of their duration and their place in the timeline of American history, all share the same basic characteristic: they transformed the United States' political, cultural, and social landscape for future generations of Americans.

Taking heed of this fundamental reality, American citizens, schools, and other institutions are increasingly emphasizing the importance of understanding our nation's history. Omnigraphics' *Defining Moments* series was created for the express purpose of meeting this growing appetite for authoritative, useful historical resources. This series will be of enduring value to anyone interested in learning more about America's past—and in understanding how those historical events continue to reverberate in the twenty-first century.

Each individual volume of *Defining Moments* provides a valuable one-stop resource for readers interested in learning about the most profound events in our nation's history. Each volume is organized into three distinct sections—Narrative Overview, Biographies, and Primary Sources.

- The **Narrative Overview** provides readers with a detailed, factual account of the origins and progression of the "defining moment" being examined. It also explores the event's lasting impact on America's political and cultural landscape.

- The **Biographies** section provides valuable biographical background on leading figures associated with the event in question. Each biography concludes with a list of sources for further information on the profiled individual.

- The **Primary Sources** section collects a wide variety of pertinent primary source materials from the era under discussion, including official documents, papers and resolutions, letters, oral histories, memoirs, editorials, and other important works.

Individually, each of these sections is a rich resource for users. Together, they comprise an authoritative, balanced, and absorbing examination of some of the most significant events in U.S. history.

Other notable features contained within each volume in the series include a glossary of important people, places, and terms; a detailed chronology featuring page references to relevant sections of the narrative; an annotated bibliography of sources for further study; an extensive general bibliography that reflects the wide range of historical sources consulted by the author; and a subject index.

Acknowledgements

This series was developed in consultation with a distinguished Advisory Board composed of public librarians, school librarians, and educators. They evaluated the series as it developed, and their comments and suggestions were invaluable throughout the production process. Any errors in this and other volumes in the series are ours alone. Following is a list of board members who contributed to the *Defining Moments* series:

Gail Beaver, M.A., M.A.L.S.
Adjunct Lecturer, University of Michigan
Ann Arbor, MI

Melissa C. Bergin, L.M.S., N.B.C.T.
Library Media Specialist, Niskayuna High School
Niskayuna, NY

Rose Davenport, M.S.L.S., Ed. Specialist
Library Media Specialist, Pershing High School Library
Detroit, MI

Karen Imarisio, A.M.L.S.
Assistant Head of Adult Services, Bloomfield Twp. Public Library
Bloomfield Hills, MI

Nancy Larsen, M.L.S., M.S. Ed.
Library Media Specialist, Clarkston High School
Clarkston, MI

Marilyn Mast, M.I.L.S.
Kingswood Campus Librarian, Cranbrook Kingswood Upper School
Bloomfield Hills, MI

Rosemary Orlando, M.L.I.S.
Library Director, St. Clair Shores Public Library
St. Clair Shores, MI

Comments and Suggestions

We welcome your comments on the *Defining Moments* series and *The Dream of America: Immigration 1870-1920,* and we also welcome suggestions for other events in U.S. history that warrant treatment in the *Defining Moments* series. Correspondence should be addressed to:

Editor, *Defining Moments*
Omnigraphics, Inc.
P.O. Box 31-1640
Detroit, MI 48231-1640
E-mail: editorial@omnigraphics.com

HOW TO USE THIS BOOK

*D*efining Moments: The Dream of America: Immigration 1870-1920 provides users with a detailed and authoritative overview of this event, as well as the principal figures involved in this pivotal episode in U.S. history. The preparation and arrangement of this volume—and all other books in the *Defining Moments* series—reflect an emphasis on providing a thorough and objective account of events that shaped our nation, presented in an easy-to-use reference work.

The Dream of America: Immigration 1870-1920 is divided into three primary sections. The first of these sections, the **Narrative Overview**, provides a detailed, factual account of the greatest sustained wave of immigration in U.S. history. It explains the economic and political forces that drove emigrants from Europe and other parts of the world, as well as the factors that made America so attractive to millions. This section also covers all aspects of the immigrants' experience, including their arduous ocean journeys, their passage through Ellis Island, and their struggles to build a better life in America. Finally, this section details America's immigration history from the 1920s through the present—including America's twenty-first century struggles with illegal immigration.

The second section, **Biographies**, provides valuable biographical background on leading figures involved in this era, including Jane Addams, the famous reformer who devoted much of her life to improving the lives of immigrants; Henry Cabot Lodge, a politician who spent years trying to reduce the flow of immigrants into the United States; and Robert Watchorn and William Williams, both of whom served memorable terms as commissioner of Ellis Island in the early 1900s. Each biography concludes with a list of sources for further information on the profiled individual.

The third section, **Primary Sources**, collects essential and illuminating documents on America's immigration history. This diverse collection includes poignant recollections of transatlantic voyages to America and arrivals at Ellis Island, muckraking reports on deplorable steerage conditions, turn-of-the-century editorials arguing for and against open immigration policies, true stories detailing the assimilation struggle that new immigrants faced, and diverse commentaries on the immigration issues confronting America in the twenty-first century.

Other valuable features in *The Dream of America: Immigration 1870-1920* include the following:

- Attribution and referencing of primary sources and other quoted material to help guide users to other valuable historical research resources.
- Glossary of Important People, Places, and Terms.
- Detailed Chronology of events with a *see reference* feature. Under this arrangement, events listed in the chronology include a reference to page numbers within the Narrative Overview wherein users can find additional information on the event in question.
- Photographs of the leading figures and major events associated with the era
- Sources for Further Study, an annotated list of noteworthy works about the movement.
- Extensive bibliography of works consulted in the creation of this book, including books, periodicals, Internet sites, and videotape materials.
- A Subject Index.

NARRATIVE OVERVIEW

PROLOGUE

The United States has long taken pride in the fact that it was founded and nurtured by brave and determined immigrants. Pilgrims, Quakers, and other early settlers of colonial America are icons of the nation's history. They were followed by millions of English, German, and Irish immigrants who helped build America's early cities, settle its vast interior, and harness its rich bounty of natural resources for economic advancement.

Once the Civil War finally drew to a close in 1865 after four years of horrible bloodshed, immigration to the United States swelled to its greatest levels yet. The period from 1870 to 1924 became the "age of immigration" in America's history books, as immigrants made the voyage to the United States by the millions. Most of them decided to uproot themselves and make a new start because of poverty and oppression in their homelands. They set their sights on the United States—rather than other parts of the world—because of the country's global reputation as a place of political and religious freedom, economic opportunity, and plentiful land and resources.

The immigrants who made the arduous journey to America during this period came from different ethnic, political, and religious backgrounds than earlier generations of immigrants. Most of the "new immigrants" came from southern and eastern Europe instead of England, Ireland, Germany, and other parts of northern and western Europe. These new arrivals included millions of Russian Jews, southern Italians, refugees from Austria-Hungary, and others carrying languages and cultural traditions that were unfamiliar and strange to the "old immigrants" and native-born Americans.

This vast tidal wave of new immigrants to America was channeled primarily through the gates of Ellis Island, a modest spit of land in New York

Harbor, a short distance from the Statue of Liberty. Fully three out of four immigrants that arrived in the United States from 1892 until World War I were processed at Ellis Island. The island thus became a symbol of the entire immigration experience for millions of Americans.

The daily procession of immigrants through Ellis Island convinced millions of Americans that immigration would forever change the nation. Some viewed this change as a positive development to be embraced. Others, though, interpreted the deluge of new arrivals as a dark threat to the nation's health, vitality, and cultural identity.

In 1906 the famed English writer H.G. Wells offered up his own impressions of Ellis Island in *The Future in America: A Search after Realities*. Wells did not take a strong stand on whether the new arrivals pouring through Ellis Island would invigorate or poison the economic, political, and cultural blood of the United States. But as he watched immigrant men, women, and children from around the world make their way through the bureaucratic maze at Ellis Island, he agreed that, one way or another, the new immigrants were sure to change America forever:

> The central hall is the key of this impression. All day long, through an intricate series of metal pens, the long procession [of new immigrants] files, step by step, bearing bundles and trunks and boxes, past this examiner and that, past the quick, alert medical officers, the tallymen and the clerks. At every point immigrants are being picked out and set aside for further medical examination, for further questions, for the busy little courts; but the main procession satisfies conditions, passes on. It is a daily procession that, with a yard of space to each, would stretch over three miles, that in any week in the year would more than equal in numbers that daily procession of the unemployed that is becoming a regular feature of the London winter, that in a year could put a cordon round London or New York of close-marching people, could populate a new Boston, that in a century—What in a century will it all amount to?
>
> On they go, from this pen to that, pen by pen, towards a desk at a little metal wicket—the gate of America.... The great majority are young men and young women, between seven-

teen and thirty, good, youthful, hopeful peasant stock. They stand in a long string, waiting to go through that wicket, with bundles, with little tin boxes, with cheap portmanteaus [suitcases], with odd packages, in pairs, in families, alone, women with children, men with strings of dependents, young couples. All day that string of human beads waits there, jerks forward, waits again; all day and every day, constantly replenished, constantly dropping the end beads through the wicket, till the units mount to hundreds and the hundreds to thousands....

Yes, Ellis Island is quietly immense. It gives one a visible image of one aspect at least of this world—the large process of filling and growing and synthesis, which is America.

"Look there!" said the Commissioner, taking me by the arm and pointing, and I saw a monster steamship far away, and already a big bulk looming up in the Narrows. "It's the *Kaiser Wilhelm der Grosse*. She's got—I forget the exact figures, but let us say—853 more for us. She'll have to keep them until Friday at the earliest. And there's more behind her, and more strung out all across the Atlantic."

In one record day this month, 21,000 immigrants came into the port of New York alone; in one week over 50,000. This year the total will be 1,200,000 souls, pouring in, finding work at once, producing no fall in wages. They start digging and building and making. Just think of the dimensions of it![1]

Notes

[1] Wells, H.G. *The Future in America: A Search after Realities.* New York and London: Harper and Bros., 1906, pp. 43-47.

1

IMMIGRATION TO AMERICA BEFORE THE CIVIL WAR

❦

We hold these truths to be self-evident, that all men are created equal, that they are men endowed by their creator with certain unalienable rights, that among these are life, liberty, and the pursuit of happiness.

—Declaration of Independence, July 4, 1776

The first people to live in North America—Native Americans—were in a very real sense immigrants themselves. Many scholars believe that the ancestors of modern Native Americans first entered the continent from Asia between 13,000 and 16,000 years ago via a thin land bridge that once ran across the Bering Sea, connecting Siberia and Alaska. Other scholars advance theories of coastal migration, in which early migrants voyaged down the Pacific coast by boat, and then moved into the continent's interior.

However these ancestors of the Native Americans arrived, they gradually spread not only across North America, but also into Central and South America. They divided into distinct tribes with unique cultural practices, religious beliefs, and methods of survival. These tribes had North America to themselves until the opening years of the seventeenth century. It was at that time that the colonial era of American history began.

Colonization and Development

The discovery of the New World and its abundant natural resources by Christopher Columbus and other explorers fired the imaginations of a wide assortment of Europeans. These people ranged from peasant farmers seeking

An engraving of a 1634 landing of English colonists on the Potomac River in Virginia.

greater economic opportunity and religious freedom to wealthy trading companies and other business interests who wanted to harvest the continent's trea-
sures of timber, fur, minerals, and land to add to their riches. These companies
became an important source of funding for colonization of the New World.

European colonization of the New World proceeded very differently in
North America than it did in Central and South America. Spain conquered the
Aztecs and other indigenous peoples who lived in Central and South America
in violent and ruthless fashion. The Spanish conquistadores then placed many
of these peoples in virtual slavery in agricultural fields and gold and silver

mines. The goods and raw materials generated by these activities were shipped back to Spain to fill the coffers of the government and the trading companies.

The first wave of European arrivals in North America, meanwhile, was more concerned with survival than conquest. These early colonists were farmers and traders rather than soldiers and explorers, and they hailed primarily from the British Empire. "Colonization required a different kind of person than the explorer—someone willing to leave the familiar homeland yet prepared to invest a lifetime in creating a new place," wrote one scholar. "Colonists [of North America] did not expect to be paid in cash but hoped to recoup their investment through cheap land and their own labor."[1]

> "Year by year, there were fewer alternatives until the critical day when only a single choice remained to be made—to emigrate or to die," wrote historian Oscar Handlin.

Other European powers tried to colonize the continent as well. But most of the French and Dutch settlements remained small because their governments could not convince large numbers of their citizens to start over in the New World (see "America's First Melting Pot," p. 11). This reality gave the British a significant advantage in colonizing North America, for many people within its fast-growing population desperately wanted to seek a different path than the impoverished one that awaited them at home. Indeed, the foundations of the earliest colonies in North America were laid primarily by English and Welsh farmers, as well as Presbyterians from the north of Ireland, the so-called Scotch-Irish. Many of these early arrivals brought their entire families with them to the New World.

Some of the early colonists were Pilgrims, Puritans, Catholics, and Quakers who braved the perilous voyage across the Atlantic so that they could practice their religious beliefs without interference from England's domineering Anglican Church. Puritans, for example, became an important force in colonial Massachusetts. Further west, William Penn and his fellow Quakers played a leading role in the development of the territory that came to be known as Pennsylvania. English Catholics, meanwhile, concentrated in colonial Maryland. In each of these places, the new immigrants gloried in setting up religious services and practices free from interference from the Anglican Church and other state-sanctioned religious authorities.

But many other immigrants were not fleeing religious persecution. Instead, these English, Welsh, and Scotch-Irish migrants were simply seeking a more independent and financially secure life than seemed possible in the British Empire. Back home, virtually all land was owned by the wealthy nobility, and opportunities for economic betterment were severely limited. To these migrants, staying in Europe meant a lifetime of financial struggle and second-class citizenship. America, on the other hand, offered the prospect of ownership of large sections of land that could be used for growing crops, raising livestock, and harvesting timber and other riches. For many, the choice was easy.

These early colonizers laid the foundations for English to become the dominant language in America. They also took the British cultural traditions that they had grown up with and planted them in American soil, where they flourished and became cornerstones of daily colonial life. Finally, these new arrivals pursued policies of diplomacy and negotiation with the Native American tribes already living in New England and further south along the Atlantic seaboard. As time passed, tensions rose between the fast-growing colonies and the tribes over fishing rights, land use, and other issues. In the worst cases, these tensions exploded into violence and murder. But the colonies continued to grow, fed by ships full of immigrants and the first-ever generations of children of European descent born on American soil.

Many of the immigrants who followed the first colonizers of the New World were warmly received, for they provided welcome help in taming the wilderness, creating fields and pastures, defending settlements from hostile Indians, and building community spirit. Even at this early era in American history, though, tensions arose between early arrivals and those who came later. Immigration, wrote one historian, stirred up anxiety and resentment among established settlers who worried that newcomers would be too dependent on them for their safety and welfare:

> Whenever a vessel anchored in the James River and a few score weary and emaciated gentlemen, worn out by three months upon the Atlantic, stumbled up the bank, the veterans who had survived nature's rigorous "seasoning" looked at one another in despair and asked: "Who is to feed them? Who is to teach them to fight the Indians, or grow tobacco, or clear the marshy lands and build a home in the malaria-infested swamps? These immigrants certainly are a problem."[2]

America's First Melting Pot

In colonial America, few towns rivaled the Dutch settlement of New Amsterdam—today known as New York City—for its mix of immigrant ethnicities. The town, perched at the mouth of the Hudson River, had been founded by the Dutch in 1625. It quickly became a base of operations for the Dutch West India Company, one of the world's most powerful trading companies during that era. But the Dutch government and company officials could not persuade many people from the Netherlands to sail for the New World, so they actively sought other nationalities to populate the town. By 1650, immigrants from numerous lands roamed the dirt streets of New Amsterdam. According to some accounts, more than a dozen languages could be heard on any given street at one time.

The presence of the Dutch outpost, though, was a source of great irritation to the British crown. England possessed much of the Atlantic seaboard to the north of New Amsterdam (in the form of the New England colonies) as well as the land to the south (the colonies of Maryland and Virginia). British officials knew that if it could take New Amsterdam for itself, it would be able to enforce its commercial regulations in the colonies more easily—and more easily defend the entire region from unfriendly armies.

Dutch administrators in New Amsterdam recognized this possibility. In 1654 Governor Peter Stuyvesant warned government officials and the Dutch West India Company that the English forces that surrounded them are "able to deprive us of the country when they please." But neither the Dutch government nor the company acted to bolster the city's defenses, and in August 1664 a large English naval force seized the city and its 1,500 inhabitants without firing a shot. The English promptly renamed the settlement New York City, and today—nearly 400 years after its founding—it remains the most ethnically diverse city in the United States.

Sources: Burrows, Edwin G., and Mike Wallace. *Gotham: A History of New York City to 1898.* Cambridge, MA: Oxford University Press, 1998.

Ellis, Edward Robb. *The Epic of New York City: A Narrative History.* New York: Marboro Books, 1966.

Servants and Slaves

Early farmers and craftsmen were joined in the New World by two other major classes of immigrants: indentured servants and slaves. Indentured servants were an important source of labor in the colonies, especially in the South. In fact, nearly half of the white immigrants who arrived in the Carolinas, Virginia, and Maryland in the seventeenth century were indentured servants. In the Chesapeake Bay region alone, about three-quarters of the immigrants who settled there in the 1600s were indentured servants.[3]

These men and women—usually young and single and always poor—agreed to provide labor for anywhere from three to seven years to a farmer or craftsman in exchange for passage to the New World and basic food and shelter in the colonies. Some contracts also promised land to servants after they fulfilled the terms of their contract.

Captured and enslaved Africans were the other major group that came across the Atlantic Ocean to North America during the colonial era. Scholars trace the beginnings of slavery of black people in North America to 1619, when a Dutch ship deposited 20 enslaved Africans on the shores of the colony in Jamestown, Virginia. In the two and a half centuries following that grim landing, an estimated 500,000 African slaves were ripped from their homelands and taken to America to harvest tobacco, pick cotton, and otherwise serve white masters. During this same period, millions of other African victims of the slave trade were forcibly taken to the West Indies, Brazil, and other parts of Central and South America, where they led lives of grim despair under Spanish and Portuguese overseers.

As the eighteenth century progressed, indentured servitude in America gradually faded in importance and slavery became more deeply entrenched. White men and women who might once have considered the path of the indentured servant or apprentice in America instead stayed in England, where the Industrial Revolution had sparked an explosion of new factories, shops, and ironworks looking for labor. Exploitation and abuse of indentured servants by masters also contributed to its decline.

Land owners and craftsmen in America, meanwhile, had determined that slaves were more profitable than indentured servants anyway. They could be treated more ruthlessly, worked harder, and kept for entire lifetimes—and they also produced a steady supply of new labor in the form of sons and daughters. Black women slaves could also be put to work in the fields—

Drawing of captured Africans being taken by slave traders for transport to America.

unlike white women, who were limited to household chores, milling, dairying, and other traditional female work by European societal traditions. Finally, contracts with indentured servants often provided for them to receive parcels of land once they fulfilled the terms of their indenture; masters were under no such obligation to give any such compensation to slaves.

These factors made slavery a big element in America's early economic development.

By the time the first census of the newly independent United States was taken in 1790, African Americans accounted for almost 20 percent of the five million people in the country. The percentage was even higher in the South, which developed a regional economy and culture that was heavily dependent on slavery over the course of the eighteenth century.

Immigration after Independence

In 1775 long-simmering resentments among the colonists over British tax policies and other heavy-handed rules imposed by the British government finally boiled over. Supporters of total independence from the British Empire took the reins of government in all thirteen colonies. They also organized militias that took up arms against British troops at the Battle of Bunker Hill, the Battle of Lexington and Concord, and in smaller skirmishes. In 1776 the American colonies made their famous Declaration of Independence from British rule, and over the course of the next five years they waged a spirited and successful war to establish their independence from the British crown. The Revolutionary War ended on the battlefield in 1781 with a major British defeat at Yorktown, Virginia. After this stunning loss at the hands of the American revolutionaries (supported by French troops), enthusiasm for the war plummeted in the British Parliament. Two years later, the two sides signed the Treaty of Paris, which formally recognized the United States of America as an independent nation.

The leadership of the newly created United States then set about meeting the challenging task of setting up governmental institutions and laws that would sustain their vision of a democratic republic. In 1787 the U.S. Constitution was passed, establishing a fundamental set of laws for the fledgling nation. Four years later a set of ten amendments to the Constitution, collectively known as the Bill of Rights, came into effect. These amendments formally established treasured American freedoms of speech, religion, and the press, among others.

As the Founding Fathers of the United States ushered these laws into being, they made several distinctions between citizens who had been born in America—the so-called "native born"—and "naturalized" citizens who earned U.S. citizenship after emigrating from a foreign land. For example, the Founding Fathers decided that only native-born Americans would be eligible to hold the office of the presidency of the United States.

But most early American political and business leaders saw immigration as necessary for the future prosperity of the young nation. Without a continued infusion of new farmers and workers, the rich soil, massive forests of timber, and valuable populations of fish and game in the American interior would remain untapped. With this in mind, the U.S. Congress passed its first naturalization law in 1790. According to this law, free white men who lived in the United States for at least two years would be eligible for citizenship.

In the first few decades of America's existence, the number of new immigrants that arrived on a yearly basis remained modest. Economic problems, the War of 1812, and the hazardous six-week journey by sea cast a shadow over the United States' drawing power during these early years. In addition,

Drawing of newly arrived immigrants boarding trains in New York City, c. 1850.

the Napoleonic Wars that wracked Europe from 1803 to 1815 made it difficult for potential immigrants to secure passage to America.

In the late 1820s and 1830s, however, immigration to the United States expanded rapidly. In the 1830s almost 600,000 immigrants arrived in America, and in the 1840s the total number of immigrants setting foot on U.S. soil reached nearly 1.75 million. By the early 1840s, New York City was accepting forty passenger ships a day—some of them carrying as many as a thousand immigrants—and other major harbors in Boston, Philadelphia, San Francisco, and Charleston were swarming with new arrivals as well.

This surge in immigration was partly due to America's growing worldwide reputation as a land of economic opportunity and political and religious freedom. But an even bigger factor was the misery that afflicted many ordinary people in Europe. For millions of people in Europe, fleeing to America seemed like the only option available to keep themselves and their families out of a lifelong pit of poverty and despair.

Reasons for Leaving

During the course of the nineteenth century, the populations in Great Britain, Russia, Austria-Hungary, and other European nations exploded. Russia's population doubled during this time, and Great Britain held four times as many people at the end of the century as it did at its beginning. This dramatic rise was fed not only by rising birth rates, but also by declining death rates due to advances in medicine and science. These surging populations put additional pressure on lands and resources that were already in short supply.

Many Europeans also moved from the countryside to the city during this era. The Industrial Revolution, which began in England in the late eighteenth century, was a huge factor in this massive population shift. The Industrial Revolution ushered in a new age of factories, long-distance transportation, and large-scale agriculture. By replacing the muscle of livestock and humans with motorized machines powered by water and fossil fuels, it pried millions of people out of farm fields and into roaring factories and mills. But for many workers in Europe, the increased economic opportunities that resulted from industrialization came at a heavy price. The corporations that owned the mines, mills, and factories of the Industrial Revolution demanded that their employees work long hours under hazardous conditions. In addition, cities struggled mightily to absorb the massive influx of new residents. Large swaths of many overcrowded industrial cities became cesspools of pollution, crime, vice, and poverty.

Conditions in rural areas, meanwhile, were scarcely better. Valuable fields and pasture lands remained in the grip of a small number of wealthy lords and businessmen who maintained spectacular estates. Peasant farmers labored mightily to survive in the shadow of the great estates, but their efforts were made much more difficult by the loss of strong young sons and daughters to the factories and mills that were sprouting across the country. And once the tide of immigration to America gained strength, it exerted a tremendous pull on those who stayed behind. "Year by year, there were fewer alternatives until the critical day when only a single choice remained to be made—to emigrate or to die," wrote Oscar Handlin in *The Uprooted*, his famous history of American immigration:

> Those who had the will to make that final decision departed. That man at the crossroads knew then that this was a mass movement. Scores of his fellows in the village, hundreds in other villages, were being swept along with him. Yet he moved alone. He went as an individual. Although entire communities

were uprooted at the same time, although the whole life of the Old World had been communal, the act of migration was individual. The very fact that the peasants were leaving was a sign of the disintegration of the old village ways. What happened beyond the crossroads, each would determine by himself.... He who turned his back upon the village at the crossroads began a long journey that his mind would forever mark as its most momentous experience.[4]

The Irish Exodus to America

No people heard the call of America as clearly as the Irish. Ireland's population had doubled between 1780 and 1840, from four million to more than eight million. But the Irish held little power over their own lives. British policies and absentee landlords kept generations of Irish families in poverty. Trapped on land they had neither the right nor the money to purchase, the Irish watched helplessly as most of their meager earnings as subsistence farmers went to pay rent and taxes. Meanwhile, the British government refused to invest in education for its Catholic Irish population or provide public aid to the poor. Instead, it devoted most of its energies to policies that attacked the Catholic faith and cultural identity of the people of Ireland.

After visiting Ireland in 1835, the French writer and sociologist Gustave de Beaumont declared that "I have seen the Indian in his forests, and the Negro in his chains, and thought, as I contemplated their pitiable condition, that I saw the very extreme of human wretchedness; but I did not then know the condition of unfortunate Ireland.... Irish misery forms a type by itself, of which neither the model nor the imitation can be found anywhere else. In all countries, more or less, paupers may be discovered; but an entire nation of paupers is what was never seen until it was shown in Ireland."[5]

About one million Irish migrated to the United States between 1814 and 1844 to escape these conditions. But the scale of Irish flight to America did not reach its peak until after 1845, when the Great Potato Famine struck. Inexpensive and easy to grow, the potato had long been the main food source for Ireland's legions of subsistence farmers. In 1845, though, the Irish potato crop was devastated by a disease called blight, and tens of thousands of people across Ireland found themselves staring into a future of abject poverty and starvation. Other failures of the all-important potato crop followed in the late

This drawing shows starving Irish peasants at the gates of a British workhouse during the Great Potato Famine.

1840s and early 1850s, creating widespread famine conditions and sparking waves of evictions of destitute farmers.

The British government took a few grudging steps to help the Irish, such as opening new poorhouses for the homeless. But they refused to implement food aid programs out of concern that they might harm English landowners and businesses. In most respects British authorities simply waited for the so-called Great Hunger to run its natural course. Some British administrators and citizens even claimed that the loss of tens of thousands of Irish people to starvation would benefit both Ireland and the larger British empire in the long run. They suggested that these victims of the famine—the poorest and most vulnerable of Ireland's people—were of no use to anyone anyway. Others, meanwhile, urged desperate Irish families to seek a new life in America. "Emigration was promoted by landlords who wished to rid their largest estates of the helpless, disease-ridden tenants," confirmed one historian.[6]

Tens of thousands of Irish men, women, and children departed for America every year during the 1840s and 1850s. A half million immigrated to the United States in the 1840s alone, accounting for almost half of all new arrivals in America that decade. Meanwhile, nearly one million countrymen succumbed to starvation back in their homeland. All told, the population in Ireland fell from 8.2 million in 1841 to 6.6 million a decade later. By 1850 there were more Irish-born people living in New York City than in Dublin, Ireland's largest city.

Irish immigrants generally congregated in New York and other port cities like Boston and Philadelphia for the simplest of reasons. They were uneducated and poor, so they did not have the resources to find work as skilled craftsmen or travel deep inland to claim land for farming. In addition, they faced hateful discrimination from Americans who made fun of their speech and customs, disrespected their work habits, and scorned their Catholic faith. This last issue was particularly troublesome for the Irish, "who were accused of placing their allegiance to the Pope before the ideals of American citizenship. Most native-born Americans, including those of northern Irish descent, were of Protestant stock; the new Irish immigrants were Catholic. In the nineteenth century, many Protestants thought of the Pope as a worldly prince who ruled vast landholdings in Italy, and his followers as subjects of an alien government."[7]

But the Irish also had several things working to their advantage in America. They knew English, which was the dominant language. In addition, they found lots of work in the factories, mills, and canneries that were sprouting up in eastern cities with the spread of the Industrial Revolution. Finally, the sheer number of Irish immigrants gave them a great deal of political influence in the cities in which they settled. As time passed, Irish politicians became mayors of cities like New York and Boston on the strength of the Irish voting bloc, and Irish dominated the employment rolls of city police departments and other public services. It took several generations, but Irish immigrants gradually fought their way up the economic ladder to positions of middle-class comfort.

German Immigrants Arrive in Large Numbers

Germans provided the other major ethnic wave that came to America in the 1840s and 1850s. In fact, Germans and Irish combined accounted for 70 percent of all foreign-born Americans by 1860. The Germans came primarily because of poor economic conditions in their native country, along with the belief that the United States offered the gateway to a better life.

Unlike the Irish, these German immigrants had to learn a new language when they reached the United States. In addition, those Germans who were Catholic or Jewish rather than Protestant had to grapple with religious bigotry. But in other respects the German immigrants' transition to America was much easier than it was for their Irish counterparts. A high percentage of German immigrants worked in skilled trades for which there was a great deal of demand. German beer brewers, butchers, bakers, cigarmakers, machinists, tailors, and cabinetmakers spread out across the Northeast and Midwest, earning wages that lifted many of their families into America's middle class.

These skilled tradesmen also assumed leadership roles in vibrant German immigrant enclaves in Milwaukee and many other Midwestern cities. In fact, German communities were so large in some villages, towns, and cities that the German language was taught alongside English in public schools. By 1880 more than 800 German-language newspapers were in circulation across the United States, and seventy of these papers were dailies.

For many Irish and German immigrants of the mid-nineteenth century, then, the promise of America was fulfilled. Sometimes it took generations for these immigrant families to lift themselves out of poverty and forge new paths of economic security and social identity. And some people never found these paths because they were waylaid by misfortune or personal failings. But for the majority, the decision to cross the Atlantic and build a new life in the United States was one that was looked back on with pride and satisfaction.

Notes

[1] Yans-McLaughlin, Virginia, and Marjorie Lightman. *Ellis Island and the Peopling of America: The Official Guide.* New York: New Press, 1997, pp. 37-38.

[2] Hansen, Marcus Lee. "The Problem of the Third Generation Immigration," *Augustana Historical Society Publications,* 1938. Quoted in Vedder, Richard, Lowell Gallaway, and Stephen Moore, "The Immigration Problem: Then and Now," *Independent Review,* Winter 2000, p. 348.

[3] Morgan, Kenneth. *Slavery and Servitude in Colonial North America.* Washington Square, NY: New York University Press, 2001, p. 8.

[4] Handlin, Oscar. *The Uprooted.* 1951. Reprint. Philadelphia: University of Pennsylvania Press, 2002, pp. 34-35.

[5] Beaumont, Gustave de. *Ireland: Social, Political, and Religious.* Translated by William Cooke Taylor. Cambridge, MA: Harvard University Press, 2006, p. 130.

[6] Meltzer, Milton. *Bound for America: The Story of the European Immigrants.* New York: Benchmark, 2001, p. 32.

[7] Yans-McLaughlin, p. 47.

2

THE GREAT WAVE

~◁◀▥∿▥▶▷~

Give me your tired, your poor,
Your huddled masses, yearning to breathe free,
The wretched refuse of your teeming shore,
Send these, the homeless, tempest-tost, to me;
I lift my lamp beside the golden door.

—Emma Lazarus (inscription at the base
of the Statue of Liberty), "The New Colossus"

Immigration to the United States slowed to a trickle during the American Civil War, which raged from 1861 to 1865. As the smoke cleared from the battlefield, however, the gates opened once again. And this time, the flood of immigrants into the United States reached its greatest heights yet. During the half-century span between the early 1870s and the early 1920s, the nation received the greatest infusion of foreign-born citizens in its entire history.

This epic era of immigration in America's history hinged in large part on massive transformations taking place within the United States itself. The rapid spread of railroad networks gave Americans the capacity to explore, settle, and develop the country's vast land holdings like never before. New machines also gave mining companies, manufacturers, and farmers tools to harvest ever-greater riches from the land. In addition, the construction and operation of railroads, factories, oil fields, steel works, lumber mills, and other elements of the industrial era required huge numbers of laborers. Immigrants and native-born Americans alike flocked to these businesses for work.

By the end of the nineteenth century, America's global reputation as a land of economic opportunity and personal reinvention had never been greater. Out

21

west, railroads and telegraph lines were shattering the distances between far-flung cities—and creating new towns and villages wherever they went. The great cities of the east, meanwhile, were frenzied beehives of financial activity that seemed to keep everyone—financiers, shopkeepers, factory managers, craftsmen, servants, and unskilled laborers—in a state of perpetual motion.

To many people around the world looking to make better lives for themselves, America shone like a beacon of hope. "My boyish imagination was aflame with America," recalled a Slovenian who immigrated to the United States in 1913 as a youth. "At that time I accepted as truth nearly everything I heard about America. I believed that a single cattleman in Texas owned more cattle than there were in the entire Balkans. And my credulity was not strained when I heard that there were gold mines in California, and trees more than a thousand years old…. In America everything was possible."[1]

> *"My boyish imagination was aflame with America," recalled one immigrant. "At that time I accepted as truth nearly everything I heard about America…. In America everything was possible."*

But unlike earlier eras in American immigration history, the men and women who followed this beacon in the late nineteenth and early twentieth centuries did not hail primarily from England, Ireland, or Germany. Rather, they came overwhelmingly from the countries of Southern and Eastern Europe, where political chaos, crushing poverty, and religious bigotry cast shadows over the lives of millions of people.

The New European Immigrant

In the post-Civil War era, the ethnic background of America's immigrants underwent a remarkable shift. Irish immigration levels dropped from 46 percent of the total in the year 1840 and 37 percent in the year 1850 to only 4.2 percent by the close of the century. The downturn in immigration from Germany, the other major source of immigrants at mid-century, was just as dramatic. In 1860, Germans accounted for 35 percent of all immigrants arriving in America. Fifty years later, only 2.7 percent of the nation's new arrivals came from Germany.[2]

But even as German and Irish immigration to the United States fell, immigration from Europe's southern and eastern regions picked up dramatically. Italians, for example, accounted for only 1.7 percent of all new arrivals in 1870. By 1910, though, nearly one in five new immigrants to America called Italy his or her homeland. An even more stunning upturn could be seen from Austria-Hungary. In 1860, only one out of 500 new immigrants to America came from there. Forty years later, the figure was one out of four.[3]

Between 1880 and 1920 about 4.2 million people left Italy for the United States, the most immigrants sent by any one country during this era. Nearly three out of four Italian immigrants were men—usually single and in their prime years as workers. And the majority of them came from southern Italy, where illiteracy, poverty, and wasteful use of natural resources had reached staggering levels. Italy in this age was dominated by its northern provinces, and its political leadership "looked down on the southerners as barbarians fit only for exploitation."[4]

Determined to better their lot in life, the men and women who emigrated from Italy were also determined to assist family members who remained in the Old Country. Unlike the English, Irish, and German immigrants who had preceded them earlier in the nineteenth century, Italians often decided against taking up permanent residence in the United States. Instead, they worked in America for a few years as construction workers, miners, or factory workers, then took their hard-won savings back to Italy to buy land, get married, and help support their families. All told, about 40 percent of emigrants from Italy during this period eventually returned to their homeland.

The people who came to America from Austria-Hungary, a nineteenth-century Eastern European empire that included numerous nationalities, did so for many of the same reasons as the Italians. These immigrants—Poles, Czechs, Germans, Ukrainians, Serbs, and other ethnic groups—were mostly landless peasants who wanted to exchange their lives of economic misery and hopelessness for something better. In their homeland, aristocratic rulers held virtually all the land and resources in an iron grip. The crumbs left over for the peasants were not enough to keep disease and hunger at bay, and they were politically powerless to change things. As a result, about 1.5 million men, women, and children fled for America from the early 1880s until the onset of World War I in 1914.

Fleeing the Pale of Settlement

Many other new arrivals from Eastern Europe were refugees from Russia. The primary emigrants from the Russian Empire in the four decades from

Widespread poverty in Italy—symbolized here by a beggar in Naples, c. 1906—convinced millions of Italians to immigrate to America.

1880 to 1920 were Jews. During this time, they came to see America—and, to a lesser degree, Great Britain, South America, and other parts of the world—as a place of refuge from the hateful bigotry and mistreatment that afflicted them in their homeland.

Hatred of Jews, known as anti-Semitism, had been a dark undercurrent in Russian society for many centuries. The czars who ruled Russia used the Jews as a scapegoat for all of the empire's problems. Many peasants, trapped in lives of poverty and bitterness by the selfish policies of the czars, embraced this myth. They took comfort in having someone to lash out against for their miseries.

The czars also passed laws that singled out Jews for persecution. In 1827, for example, Czar Nicholas I imposed a statute requiring Jewish communities to surrender groups of young men for 25-year stints in the Russian Army. The czar believed that military indoctrination would gradually lead these conscripts, known as Cantonists, to forsake Judaism and give their highest loyalty to the Russian state.

The most repressive law imposed on the Jews of Russia, however, was a 1791 decree by Czar Catherine II that herded most Jews into a region that came to be known as the Pale of Settlement. This territory on the western edge of the empire served as a quarantine center of sorts. It was designed to keep the Russian population that lived in the other 96 percent of the empire's land from becoming contaminated by contact with people of the Jewish faith. Jews living within the Pale of Settlement were permitted to work as bakers, cabinetmakers, innkeepers, and in other occupations, but they paid much higher taxes than non-Jews and were forbidden from leasing land or owning some other types of business enterprises.

Despite being trapped in this ugly anti-Semitic environment, the Jewish population in the Pale rose from one million at the beginning of the nineteenth century to four million by 1880. In 1881, though, Czar Alexander II was assassinated and Jews were widely—and falsely—blamed for plotting his death. Waves of *pogroms*—anti-Jewish riots—broke out all across the Pale of Settlement. Thousands of innocent Jews were murdered in this mob violence, but the royal government refused to intervene. In fact, they seized on the anger of the peasants to impose new restrictions on Jewish rights.

In 1882 half a million Jews living in rural parts of the Pale were evicted from their homes and forced to relocate to towns or villages, called *shtetls*, within the territory. Their homes and property were taken over by already

This 1919 demonstration in London was organized to protest deadly pogroms being waged against Jews in eastern Europe.

powerful landlords. Around this same time, virtually all Jews across Russia who had been living outside of the Pale—including 20,000 in Moscow—were expelled from their homes and driven into the area, sometimes in chains. Overcrowding in the Pale's cities worsened, which heightened longstanding problems of hunger and disease. Jewish merchants and craftsmen, meanwhile, watched helplessly as their businesses withered and died.

All of these factors led tens of thousands of Jews to look for lands outside of Russia where they could raise their families and tend their businesses in peace. Between 1881 and 1914, an estimated two million Jews fled the Pale of Settlement for the United States. They were joined by hundreds of thousands of Jews from other parts of Eastern Europe who also faced discrimination and harassment because of their faith. By the early 1920s, more than three million Jews had left Eastern Europe, and most of them had chosen the United States as their new home.

Most of these Jewish emigrants from Eastern Europe settled in the cities of America's east coast, and especially in New York City. In 1880, an estimated 250,000 Jews lived in the United States, and fewer than one out of four of them hailed from Eastern Europe. By 1910 about 1.4 million Jews from Eastern Europe were living in New York City alone—approximately 25 percent of the city's entire population.

From All Corners of the World

These emigrants from Russia, Italy, and Austria-Hungary were joined by smaller numbers of new arrivals from virtually every other corner of the globe. Between 1860 and 1920, about two million Scandinavians—natives of Sweden, Norway, and Denmark—came to the United States. Most of them settled in the Midwest, where they farmed, opened small shops, and worked in the factories, mills, and stockyards of Chicago, Minneapolis, Detroit, and other growing cities.

In the Western states and territories, meanwhile, many businesses became dependent on the labor of Chinese and Mexican immigrants. In a thirty-year period beginning around 1850, an estimated 300,000 Chinese came to America. The vast majority of these immigrants were men, and they became highly prized by employers in California for being both industrious and cheap to hire. In October 1865 Leland Stanford, the powerful president of the Central Pacific Railroad, told U.S. President Andrew Johnson that construction of America's first transcontinental railroad—begun in 1863 and completed in 1869—was heavily dependent on Chinese laborers. "A large majority of the white laboring class on the Pacific Coast find more profitable and congenial employment in mining and agricultural pursuits, than in railroad work," wrote Stanford. "The greater portion of the laborers employed by us are Chinese who constitute a large element in the population of California. Without them it would be impossible to complete the western portion of this great national enterprise within the time required by the Acts of Congress."[5]

The post-Civil War United States already had a significant ethnic Mexican population because of its annexation of Texas, California, and all the land in between in the 1840s. This territory had previously been held by Mexico, so when the United States claimed the lands after winning the Mexican-American War in 1848, thousands of Mexican families suddenly found themselves living under a new government. As one historical account of these

This passport belonged to the author's paternal grandfather, who immigrated to the United States from Sweden in 1924.

events noted, "the first Mexicans to become part of the United States never crossed any border. Instead, the border crossed them."[6]

Mexicans did not enter the United States in huge numbers in the second half of the nineteenth century. Troubled by news of rampant discrimination and lack of economic opportunity faced by Mexican Americans across the border, many did not see the United States in the same positive light as did Eastern Europeans. In the opening years of the twentieth century, though, political upheaval in Mexico and a surging U.S. economy convinced thousands of Mexicans to build new lives in America. From 1910 to 1930, the number of Mexican immigrants counted by the U.S. census tripled from 200,000 to 600,000. The actual number was probably far greater, though, for many immigrants crossed the 2,000-mile-long border into the United States illegally. But not all Mexicans stayed in America. The porous border and the relatively short journey back to Mexico led many Mexican immigrants—both legal and undocumented—to stay only a few years before returning home.

Finally, the United States received comparatively small numbers of emigrants from numerous other nations during the great immigration wave of 1870-1920. French-Canadians, Greeks, French, Spaniards, Japanese, Koreans, Filipinos, Syrians, and immigrants from other lands all came through America's gates during this era. Some gathered in tight-knit ethnic communities, while others struck out on their own and eagerly shed their ethnic culture to become "Americanized." But whatever their choice, they all came for the same reason: to build better lives for themselves and their loved ones.

Notes

[1] Chermayeff, Ivan, Fred Wasserman, and Mary J. Shapiro. *Ellis Island: An Illustrated History of the Immigrant Experience.* New York: Macmillan, 1991, p. 24.

[2] U.S. Census Bureau. *Immigrants and Their Children, 1920.* Washington, DC: Census Bureau, 1927.

[3] Ibid.

[4] Meltzer, Milton. *Bound for America: The Story of the European Immigrants.* New York: Benchmark, 2002, p. 54.

[5] Quoted in Kraus, George. "Chinese Laborers and the Construction of the Central Pacific Railroad," *Utah Historical Quarterly,* 37, no. 1, winter 1969, p. 41.

[6] "Mexican Immigration." Library of Congress, American Memory Learning Page, n.d. http://memory.loc.gov/learn/features/immig/mexican2.html.

3

THE VOYAGE TO AMERICA

━◁◫〕ᶇ〔◫▷━

We went steerage.... There were a lot of children, a lot of grownups, a lot of men, a lot of women. People didn't even talk to each other they were so miserable and we always huddled together and it was very, very hard, very bad.

—Romanian Jew who immigrated to America in 1905

For immigrants, the long process of establishing new lives in the United States began with leaving old lives behind. The act of leaving, though, was usually a difficult one. Emigrating from one's native country involved saying goodbye—possibly forever—to friends, family, and places that were dear to the emigrant's heart. And the journey itself was physically demanding and spiritually exhausting for millions.

An Agonizing Choice

Poverty, political repression, and religious persecution riddled Europe from the 1870s through World War I. Meanwhile, America's reputation as a nation of cheap land and stunning riches continued to grow. As one history of U.S. immigration commented, the peoples of Europe recognized that "in America there were still frontiers to explore, room to expand, new directions to try."[1]

Letters from friends and family members who had found success after immigrating to the United States contributed mightily to the decisions of struggling Europeans to build new lives across the Atlantic. "I wish you to come to America," declared one Polish immigrant in a 1906 letter to family members he had left behind. "Up to the present I am doing very well here, and I have no intention of going to our country, because [in Poland] I experienced only misery and poverty, and now I live better than a lord."[2]

31

Yet despite such encouragement, leaving one's homeland was a difficult decision for many immigrants. The emotional strain was cushioned somewhat for immigrants who were able to book passage with other friends and family members. But most of the immigrants were young men and women who traveled by themselves. For these brave but frightened voyagers, saying goodbye to loved ones was an emotional ordeal. A Lithuanian immigrant who came to America in 1899 recalled that "the day I left home, my mother came with me to the railroad station. When we said goodbye, she said it was just like seeing me go into my casket. I never saw her again."[3]

> *"There is neither breathing space below nor deck room above, and the 900 steerage passengers ... are positively packed like cattle," reported Edward Steiner.*

Millions of immigrants experienced similar partings. One Greek immigrant who came to America in 1911 as a 16-year-old recalled saying good-bye to his father in the shadow of the ocean liner that would take him away. "We shake hands, and he say, 'Theo, I never say to you go or not go. I'm very proud that you make up your own mind to go to America. I know you're going to have a better life in America than we have here.' Because there my father was a hardworking man, working day and night. He was in the fish business, in fishing boats with the nets. And then I left, and he was crying. He was crying. And you know how I felt when I left my home, my father and my mother? Terrible, terrible. That's how I felt."[4]

Immigration to America, then, was not for the faint of heart. Travelers to the United States not only had to possess money for passage and clothing for warmth, but large quantities of bravery and determination. The immigrants who came to America "had to possess the will to voluntarily uproot themselves from home and family, the strength to endure the often harsh transition from the familiar to the strange, and, above all, the imagination even to dream of a better life."[5]

Leaving Home

Once the decision had been made to emigrate from the Old Country, the first step for immigrants was to secure money to buy passage on one of the steamships that could carry them across the Atlantic to the United States. Most individuals and families from Eastern Europe could not afford first-class or even second-class tickets. Instead, they bought tickets in "steerage"—dark and cramped quarters deep in the innards of the ships, adjacent to the vessel's steerage system. Immigrants who left for America in family groups also sold

Greek immigrants embarking on small boats that will take them to steamers bound for the United States.

their homes, land, and other possessions in order to gather as much money as possible for relocation.

Immigrants then journeyed to the leading European seaports used by the passenger line companies. Limited funds and transportation options forced many southern and eastern Europeans to walk to the ports from far-away towns and farms, crossing rivers, mountains, and forests. In some cases, these journeys could take several weeks and tax the strength of even the hardiest young men and women.

The leading ports in Europe for immigration were located in Naples, Italy; Liverpool, England; Bremen, Germany; and Hamburg, Germany. By 1907 about

60 percent of all immigrants to America began their voyages at these ports. Other leading European ports used by the passenger line companies included Rotterdam, Netherlands; Gdansk (in modern-day Poland); and Trieste, Italy.

Ports of Departure

The leading shipping companies took full economic advantage of this massive population shift from Europe to the United States. They were already making good money by transporting huge quantities of cotton, tobacco, lumber, coal, furs, and other valuable cargo from America to European markets. With the explosion in the immigrant transport trade, they were able to use human cargo to tally even greater profits on the return trip to American ports.

As part of their efforts to lure America-bound individuals and families to their ships, shipping lines sent agents all across Europe to sell tickets. Armed with promotional brochures created by shipping lines and U.S. railroad companies, these agents became a leading source of the "America's streets are paved with gold" mythology that swept like wildfire through European farmhouses, villages, and cities. Meanwhile, several major shipping lines built hotels, dormitories, and other facilities for steerage passengers who arrived at ports before their ships were ready to sail. The Hamburg-America Line, for example, built a village along Hamburg's harbor that was capable of housing up to 5,000 passengers. It even had two churches and a synagogue.

Shipping companies also opened medical clinics to check on the health of emigrants holding steerage tickets before they boarded. Within these facilities, ticket-holders were required to take antiseptic baths and turn their baggage over for fumigation. They also submitted to medical examinations carried out by doctors employed by the shipping lines. These measures, though, were taken to protect the profits of the shipping lines, not out of concern for the health and well-being of the steerage passengers. The U.S. Immigration Service fined shipping lines $100 for each prospective immigrant that it rejected, so the steamship companies made a special effort to identify—and turn away—anyone who appeared to be in poor health.

American authorities also imposed laws that required the shipping companies to compile a formal list of passengers, including their name, point of origin, and other basic information. This list, known as the ship's manifest, served as an inventory of the ship's human cargo. It became one of the most important pieces of documentation in the entire immigration process, for

Norwegian immigrants to America prepare to leave port, c. 1905.

U.S. customs officials used it to keep track of the thousands of immigrants who were pouring into America on a daily basis.

"Positively Packed Like Cattle"

Once the passenger liners departed Europe for the open Atlantic, the experience of the immigrants varied enormously. Prior to the advent of steamships, the voyage to America under sail could last as long as three or four weeks, depending on the quality of the ship and the weather conditions it encountered (in colonial times, the trips could take even longer). But when steam engines became sophisticated enough to power trans-Atlantic ships, they quickly became immigration's workhorse. In 1856, for example, fewer than 5 percent of immigrants reached America via steam-powered ships. Less than a decade later, one out of three immigrants were carried to the United States by steam. By the 1880s, all major passenger lines relied exclusively on steam-powered fleets, and Atlantic crossings had been reduced to seven to ten days by the end of the nineteenth century.

On board these ships, meanwhile, conditions varied enormously, depending on the morals of the captain and crew, the policies of the ships' owners, and the type of ticket that the immigrant held. For the few immigrants who could afford first-class or even second-class passage, the voyage could be downright pleasant. These travelers were housed in cabins that were clean—or even luxurious in first-class suites—and slept on beds dressed in fresh linens. They also dined well and were treated with courtesy by attentive ship stewards.

Most immigrants, though, could only afford tickets in steerage. And for many immigrants making the voyage between 1870 and 1920, the crossing turned into a living hell of stifling heat (in summer), bone-chilling cold (in winter), overcrowded conditions, weeping children, horrid food, creeping vermin, and seasickness-induced nausea (see "The 'Horrors' of Steerage," p. 156). Even on luxurious passenger liners like the *Kaiser Wilhelm II*, steerage conditions were terrible. "There is neither breathing space below nor deck room above, and the 900 steerage passengers ... are positively packed like cattle," reported immigrant advocate Edward Steiner in his 1906 book *On the Trail of the Immigrant*. "On the whole, the steerage of the modern ship ought to be condemned as unfit for the transportation of human beings."[6]

On most boats, overcrowding was the least of the immigrants' worries. Sickness and disease blossomed in steerage, as toilet facilities and fresh water were extremely limited—and those that existed were often left untended by the crew until the ship was in sight of the U.S. coast. Other accommodations were equally terrible. Mattresses often consisted of nothing more than burlap bags full of lice-infested straw or seaweed, and passengers were given no storage space for their baggage. Instead, they had to cram all of their worldly possessions in the corners of their small sleeping berths.

Stormy seas brought epidemics of vomiting inside the claustrophobic confines of steerage. Nausea from seasickness was a common problem in

Steerage passengers rested on deck whenever possible so as to escape the miserable conditions in the steerage sections of immigrant ships.

steerage even in calm seas. When conditions turned rough, the misery quickly spread. "Hundreds of people had vomiting fits" during a storm, recalled one Jewish immigrant. "I wanted to escape from that inferno but no sooner had I thrust my head forward from the lower bunk than someone above me vomited straight upon my head."[7]

Meals for steerage passengers were handed out in cafeteria rooms that sometimes doubled as sleeping quarters for unfortunate immigrants. During mealtime, passengers stood in shuffling lines to receive hastily prepared food that often tasted bad and was of little nutritional value. And unlike first- and second-class passengers, people in steerage were expected to supply their own plates, cups, and eating utensils. Yet keeping these mess kits clean between meals was next to impossible, given the crowds that perpetually surrounded the few wash basins in steerage.

Predatory Sailors and Nighttime Fears

Occasionally, the well-fed travelers who freely roamed the decks above steerage would take pity on the hungry immigrants below. One Romanian

Jew who came to America in 1905 as a young child recalled that when she and her fellow steerage passengers were permitted to go out on deck, "people from upstairs, first class and second class, would look down on us, and they would feel sorry for us, and many times they would throw down an orange, or apples, or candy. We, the children, would all stand by and this one would catch this and this one would catch that. You were lucky to get something."[8]

But steerage passengers received no help from their wealthier brethren in warding off the lawlessness that sometimes pervaded the steerage conditions. Women immigrants frequently had to fight off unwanted sexual advances from crew members or other passengers, and incidents of rape undoubtedly occurred on many voyages. Petty thefts and outbreaks of violence also were problems in steerage, especially when frustrations mounted or ethnic groups armed with a historic distrust of one another were forced to share close quarters.

For some immigrants, though, the brutalities and indignities of the day paled next to the fears that blossomed at night. As one young immigrant recalled, "The perils of the sea were not minimized in the imaginations of us inexperienced voyagers. The captain and his officers ate their dinners, smoked their pipes and slept soundly in their turns, while we frightened emigrants turned our faces to the wall and awaited our watery graves."[9]

This misery was further compounded by a level of boredom that reached stupefying levels during the long days and nights at sea. Recreational opportunities in steerage were extremely limited. Many travelers tried to fill the hours with cards, music, or religious services, but other diversions were in very short supply. For example, reading was difficult for even literate immigrants (few of them had the baggage space to carry books on board, anyway). In addition, language differences made it impossible for many neighbors in steerage to carry on even the simplest of conversations.

As a result, many steerage passengers spent hours simply lying in their uncomfortable bunks and wishing for an end to their suffering. "They'd lie there," wrote historian Oscar Handlin, "seafaring adventurers out to discover new continents, amidst the retching, noisome stench, the stomach-turning filth of hundreds of bodies confined to close quarters. Many nights, and many days that were indistinguishable from nights, they could see, by the sickly light of swinging lanterns, the creaking ugly timbers crowding in about them; they could hear the sounds of men in uneasy silence, of children in fitful rest;

A crowded ship full of European immigrants to America, 1906.

everywhere they could sense the menace of hostile winds and waves, of indifferent companions, of repressed passions."[10]

Efforts to Reform Steerage

Horror stories about steerage filtered through American society for decades. New arrivals in America compared their tales of woe with friends and family members who had come in earlier years. Leading newspapers in New York, Chicago, and elsewhere joined foreign-language newspapers across the country in denouncing the dangerous and dehumanizing conditions.

One of the most effective arguments used by immigration advocates who wanted to reform steerage—or abolish it altogether—focused on the physical and emotional health of new arrivals. They argued that voyages in steerage took such a heavy toll on immigrants that their capacity to take care of them-

The Idealism of the Immigrant

Edward Steiner was one of the millions of eastern Europeans who immigrated to the United States during the latter part of the nineteenth century. Born into a Jewish family in the Austro-Hungarian Empire (now the Czech Republic), Steiner came to the United States in the late 1880s. He eventually converted to Christianity. After spending some time as a minister, he became a professor of Christianity at Grinnell College in Grinnell, Iowa.

Steiner also was a lifelong advocate for immigrants, and he wrote numerous books on the subject. In his 1914 memoir *From Alien to Citizen,* he acknowledged, that for many immigrants, America did not live up to the mythology that surrounded it. He warned that new arrivals would face many dangers and injustices. But he also professed his love for his adopted country:

> I should like the entrance into the United States to be a poem to all who come, and not the horrible tragedy into which it often resolves itself when the first ecstasy is over. All the way across the sea I would make of every ship a school, with such fair comforts as men are entitled to, for their money.

> I should like to teach them that they may enter without fear and without uttering a lie, so that those at the gate might know that these new comers are human, and treat them as such, so long as they conduct themselves properly.

> I should like to teach the strangers that there is a fair reward for hard struggle and an honest living wage for an honest day's

selves—and avoid becoming dependent on aid from the state for their survival—was often compromised once they reached America's shores.

Other reformers argued that negative experiences in steerage permanently poisoned the immigrants' vision of the United States—and thus made it more difficult to mold them into law-abiding, loyal Americans. This same concern was voiced by an investigator for the U.S. Immigration Commission in 1908. He charged that some immigrants reach "journey's work. That they must guard their health by abstinence from intoxicating drink, and I should like to prohibit its sale on board of ship and everywhere else. For to the immigrants, the ignorant immigrants, alcohol is a lying curse. They believe that it strengthens and that no hard labour can be done without it.

I should like to tell them also that their health will be guarded in mines and factories and that their bodies and souls have value to man and to God.

I should like to point to the Goddess of Liberty and say that she welcomes all who come in her name, that she guarantees freedom to all who obey law, that our law is always reasonable and that, if it is a burden, it falls upon the shoulders of rich and poor alike.

I should like to tell them that they have nothing to fear in this country except their own frailties, that there are no barriers here but their own clannishness and that the way to the best is open to all who walk reverently.

This and more I should like to be able to teach; fragments of it I have taught, more of it than many of them will find true, I fear. But to me so much of it has been true that I should like to have all men find it so. I have suffered much here, I have gone the whole scale of hunger, sorrow and despair; yet I say it again and again, Holy America! Holy America!

Source: Steiner, Edward. *From Alien to Citizen: The Story of My Life in America.* New York: Fleming H. Revell, 1914, pp. 43-44.

end with a mind unfit for healthy wholesome impressions and with a body weakened and unfit for the hardships . . . involved in the beginning of life in a new land."[11]

For a long time, though, the reformers made little headway in their efforts. The powerful steamship companies used their connections in Congress to torpedo most reform legislation. Some companies even distorted the motives of reformers. They publicly charged reformers with being *enemies* of immigration because their reforms would have reduced the number of immigrants that could be legally placed on each vessel.

Steerage conditions did not improve significantly until the 1910s. During this period, the United States finally passed legislation that curbed some of the worst abuses. But an even bigger factor may have been the competition for immigrants' money. Shipping companies began to see the competitive advantages of offering decent lodging, food, and service to all passengers, not just the wealthy and middle-class. When they ordered new vessels from shipyards, steerage sections were not even included in some cases. Instead, the space was filled with individual cabins that slept four or six people. These "third-class" accommodations were still plain and cramped, but they were a huge improvement over the old steerage dormitories. The improvement in conditions made it easier for immigrants to play cards, play with children, and even enjoy occasional music from talented fiddlers or other musicians making the voyage. In addition, some shipping lines started offering third-class passengers much better food—and serving the meals in well-lit dining rooms with plates and flatware supplied by the lines themselves.

For immigrants fortunate enough to book passage on one of these ships, the voyage to America was not the miserable nightmare that it had been for earlier generations. But many of the old ships were kept in service as well, so steerage remained a grim reality for many.

Notes

[1] Brownstone, David M., Irene M. Franck, and Douglass Brownstone. *Island of Hope, Island of Tears.* New York: MetroBooks, 2003, p. 10.

[2] Chermayeff, Ivan, Fred Wasserman, and Mary J. Shapiro. *Ellis Island: An Illustrated History of the Immigrant Experience.* New York: Macmillan, 1991, p. 26.

[3] Chermayeff et al, p. 29.

[4] Interview with Theodore Spako. *Ellis Island Interviews: In Their Own Words.* By Peter Morton Coan. New York: Facts on File, 1997, p. 277.

[5] *Immigrants: The New Americans.* Editors of Time-Life Books. New York: Time-Life, 1999, p. 21.

[6] Steiner, Edward. *On the Trail of the Immigrant.* New York: Fleming H. Revell, 1906, p. 35.

[7] Quoted in Sorin, Gerald. *The Jewish People in America. Vol. III: A Time for Building, The Third Migration, 1880-1920.* Baltimore: Johns Hopkins University Press, 1992, p. 46.

[8] Interview with Esther Gidiwicz. *Ellis Island Interviews: In Their Own Words.* By Peter Morton Coan. New York: Facts on File, 1997, p. 326.

[9] Chermayeff, et al, pp. 42-43.

[10] Handlin, Oscar. *The Uprooted: The Epic Story of the Great Migrations that Made the American People.* 1952. Reprint. Philadelphia: University of Pennsylvania Press, 2002, pp. 46-47.

[11] Quoted in Sorin, Gerald. *The Jewish People in America. Vol. III: A Time for Building, The Third Migration, 1880-1920.* Baltimore: Johns Hopkins University Press, 1992, p. 46.

4

ELLIS ISLAND

Ellis Island is the nations' gateway to the promised land.
There is not another such to be found anywhere.

—Jacob Riis, 1903

For immigrants to America, completing the voyage to U.S. shores was only the first step in their quest for a better life. The next hurdle was to gain official approval to enter the United States. Most prospective immigrants passed this test and promptly entered the great and turbulent stream of America's industrial age. But some immigrants were refused entry into the United States, and when the gate was closed to these men and women, scenes of fury and heartbreak often ensued.

Castle Garden

Many American ports became destinations for European immigrants during the course of the nineteenth century. But New York City was by far the nation's largest seaport. The city had developed major shipping lanes across the Atlantic Ocean with various European markets, and its factories and retail businesses required huge numbers of workers. The city also ranked as a central hub of the nation's fast-growing railroad network. By the 1870s, New Yorkers could use trains to reach every corner of the country, from the mine fields of Colorado and stockyards of Chicago to the farms and forests of the Upper Midwest and Deep South. Even the orchards of California were in reach. All of these attributes made New York City the leading gateway into America for European immigrants.

Wooden engraving showing immigrants being processed at Castle Garden.

For many years, New York City—like all other major American port cities—did not maintain any sort of immigration depot to check new arrivals. After all, neither the city nor the state nor the federal government had passed any immigration laws that needed to be enforced. When a passenger ship arrived in New York's harbor, the passengers simply disembarked, passed through customs, and then vanished into the bustle and chaos of the city.

In the early 1850s, however, social reformers convinced city leaders to open an immigration depot at Castle Garden, a massive stone building located on a small island off the southwest tip of Manhattan. Castle Garden, which opened in August 1855, was the first immigration landing station in the country. But it was not primarily intended to inspect the health and background of incoming arrivals. Rather, Castle Garden was designed as a sanctuary. Inside its walls, immigrants could be protected from the thieves, pimps, and con artists who skulked around the docks, preying on innocent and trusting newcomers.

In the thirty-five years that Castle Garden was in operation, it registered over eight million immigrants. Within the facility, these new arrivals were able to exchange foreign currency for U.S. dollars, purchase tickets on railroads and steamboats to other parts of the country, and obtain information on employment and housing options around the city.

As time passed, though, operations at Castle Garden slowly fell apart. Local boardinghouse operators and factory owners bribed employees to send immigrants their way, then took advantage of the immigrants to line their own pockets. Other employees who secured their jobs through political connections were lazy or incompetent. Funding for upkeep of Castle Garden, meanwhile, was completely inadequate, especially as the number of immigrants coming through the facility steadily rose in the 1870s and 1880s. One Russian Jew who was processed at Castle Garden in the early 1880s recalled that overcrowding was so bad that "there was simply nowhere to sit by day, or any place to lie down at night—not even on the bare floor.... [The] filth was unendurable, so many packages, pillows, featherbeds and foul clothing (often just plain rags) that each immigrant had dragged with him over the seas and clung to as if they were precious—all of this provided great opportunity for vermin, those filthy little beasts, that crawled about freely and openly over the clutter and made life disagreeable."[1]

"There were many heartbreaking scenes on Ellis Island," recalled New York Mayor Fiorello La Guardia. *"I never managed during the three years I worked there to become callous to the mental anguish, the disappointment and the despair I witnessed almost daily."*

Federal Authorities Step In

At the same time that corruption and neglect was eating away at Castle Garden, the American public was expressing growing anxiety about the deluge of immigrants pouring into the United States every year. Some people believed that the federal government needed to step in and give arriving immigrants more assistance in getting their bearings. Others believed that the nation needed to keep out "undesirable" immigrants who, they charged, posed a threat to workers' wages, public health and safety, and "American" political and social ideals.

The calls for federal regulation of immigration, then, were prompted by wildly different concerns. Together, however, they led Congress to pass the first significant federal immigration laws in the early 1880s. The most infamous of these laws was the 1882 Chinese Exclusion Act, a racist piece of legislation that closed the door on most emigrants from China. A few years later, Treasury Secretary William Windom bluntly informed the State of New York

Other Immigration Gateways

New York's Ellis Island absorbed most of the immigration flow from 1870 through 1920, but other port cities scattered across the United States became important gateways as well. The second-busiest port during this era was located in Boston. Irish immigrants voyaged to Boston in huge numbers throughout the second half of the nineteenth century, and they were joined at the turn of the century by Italians, Greeks, Portuguese, Russian Jews, and other groups. Other major processing centers in the east during this era included Baltimore and Philadelphia.

Over on the west coast, the leading processing center for immigrants was San Francisco's Angel Island. This facility processed applicants from Japan, China, the Philippines, and other parts of Asia. Applicants from China were subjected to the greatest restrictions at Angel Island. Emigrants from other Asian nations were quickly inspected and approved, but Chinese applicants were often held in detention for weeks or months and subjected to intense grilling from interviewers. This poor treatment was a legacy of the 1882 Chinese Exclusion Act, which barred Chinese from entering the country unless they were merchants, government officials, students, teachers, visitors, or U.S. citizens.

that Castle Garden would not longer be needed after April 1890, because the federal government was going to assume control of immigration in New York and every other U.S. port.

The U.S. government gave serious consideration to putting its New York immigration facilities on Bedloe's Island, which was home to the famous Statue of Liberty. But some people opposed turning the site of the Statue of Liberty—which had been formally dedicated only a few years earlier, in 1886—into an immigration station. They worried that the statue's appearance and symbolic value might be tarnished if thousands of immigrants and immigration officials were swarming around its feet every day.

A congressional committee was appointed to study the issue. The committee decided to locate the federal immigration facilities on Ellis Island. This small piece of land was situated next door to Bedloe's Island in the southwest quadrant of New York Harbor, and it was only a short ferry ride away from the city docks.

Readying Ellis Island for Service

The island's namesake was Samuel Ellis, who had owned the island for a number of years during the late eighteenth century. The federal government purchased the island from Ellis in 1808 and converted it into a military installation called Fort Gibson. The fort included a munitions storehouse and a barracks for both the army and navy. It was even used to execute convicted pirates. After the Civil War, though, the U.S. military stopped using the island as a military post. It became a minor, almost forgotten, storehouse for munitions.

The federal decision to house its central immigration processing center at Ellis Island returned the island to prominence. But readying Ellis Island for its new purpose was a difficult task. Since the island was too small to handle the numbers of immigrants that were passing through New York on a daily basis, officials dumped huge quantities of landfill around the perimeter to double its size. They also constructed new buildings, built new dock facilities, and dredged a deep channel so larger vessels could reach its shores. Meanwhile, state officials were so angry over losing their authority over immigration that they stubbornly refused to let federal authorities use Castle Garden until Ellis Island was ready. The federal Bureau of Immigration was forced to operate for nearly two years in temporary facilities on the mainland.

The federal immigration station on Ellis Island finally opened on January 1, 1892. It operated for only five years, though, before a major fire ripped through the station. This blaze destroyed valuable historical records of Ellis Island's first five years of existence, as well as many records from Castle Garden. The fire burned down the wood buildings so swiftly that authorities decided to use brick in rebuilding the Ellis Island facilities. Besides offices and examination rooms, these facilities eventually came to include a massive dining hall, bathhouse and laundry, dormitories, a hospital, and even an electric power plant.

Gateway to America

In the first thirty-two years after Ellis Island opened its doors, the facility processed about twelve million men, women, and children—about 75 percent of all immigrants who entered the United States during that time. Immi-

The Statue of Liberty

Head of the Statue of Liberty during construction in Paris in the early 1880s.

The nation of France presented the Statue of Liberty to the United States as a gift and gesture of friendship in the 1880s. France originally intended to turn the statue over to the United States in 1876 to commemorate the centennial of the American Declaration of Independence. But construction of the monument ran into difficulties almost from the outset. The United States had agreed to provide the pedestal for the statue using private contributions, but lack of funding delayed completion of the pedestal for several years. In France, meanwhile, sculptor Frederic-Auguste Bartholdi had to work closely with engineers to make sure that the massive copper sculpture he envisioned would not topple over in bad weather or because of structural design flaws. Bartholdi also had to make certain that he would be able to re-assemble the various pieces of the statue after they were transported to New York.

Eventually, though, the ambitious project came together. In April 1886 the United States announced that it had completed construction of the pedestal. The statue, which had been completed in July 1884, was then shipped to its final destination. It made the voyage in more than 350 massive pieces, which were then re-assembled by Bartholdi. The Statue of Liberty was then formally dedicated on October 28, 1886, in a celebration attended by thousands of Americans.

Since that time, the Statue of Liberty has become one of America's most enduring national symbols of hope and freedom. It is now managed by the National Park Service, and its operation and upkeep are paid for with the help of the private Statue of Liberty-Ellis Island Foundation.

gration officials at Ellis Island rarely rejected applicants for entrance. For every person who was rejected at Ellis Island, another fifty were allowed to pass through the station and begin a new life in the United States.

Ellis Island thus became a powerful symbol of the end of the immigrant's journey to America—and of the immigrant's arrival in a land of fabled riches and opportunities (see "A Long and Difficult Journey," p. 163). Millions of people who came to America from 1892 to 1924 held warm and powerful memories of Ellis Island. Years after arriving on America's shores, these immigrants keenly remembered the thrill of excitement they felt when they first entered New York Harbor and spotted Ellis Island and the neighboring Statue of Liberty. Similarly, the moment when they left Ellis Island and set foot on America's mainland—oftentimes while being embraced by joyful loved ones—remained a treasured memory for millions of immigrants.

But the words "Ellis Island" also conjured up darker memories, for the hours that immigrants spent at the station between arrival and departure were ones of fear and anxiety. The tension among immigrants waiting to see if they would be accepted into America sometimes became almost unbearable. And immigrants who learned that they had been rejected and would have to return to Europe were emotionally crushed by the news. "There were many heartbreaking scenes on Ellis Island," recalled New York Mayor Fiorello La Guardia, who as a young man worked as a translator at the station. "I never managed during the three years I worked there to become callous to the mental anguish, the disappointment and the despair I witnessed almost daily."[2]

A Fateful Exam

Not all immigrants to the United States were required to go to Ellis Island. Once a ship tied up at the city's docks, its first- and second-class passengers only had to pass a brief shipboard examination conducted by a federal medical officer. They were then free to walk off the ship on to the mainland, pass through customs, and begin their lives in America.

Ellis Island existed for the *rest* of the immigrants—the brave but poor Europeans who had reached the United States via tickets in steerage. When immigrant ships docked at the city harbor, all steerage passengers were placed on ferries that took them to Ellis Island. They were then ushered into the station itself to await the exams and interviews that would determine the future course of their lives.

An Ellis Island inspector examines the eyes of an immigrant, c. 1913.

The first step in the process was a brief physical examination conducted by doctors from the U.S. Public Health Service. Immigrants then presented their medical inspection cards to another doctor, who reviewed and stamped it. Individuals then entered examination rooms where they underwent much more extensive physical examinations. Doctors made special efforts to detect cases of contagious disease such as tuberculosis and favus, a common skin disease of that era.

The next hurdle for immigrants was an examination for trachoma, a disease of the eye. This highly contagious disease could lead to blindness and other eye problems, so authorities were extremely vigilant in looking for trachoma carriers. In some cases, examiners simply used their fingers to pull back the eyelids of immigrants and check for signs of infection. But many immigrants were forced to submit to doctors who used hairpins or buttonhooks—a metal instrument usually used to button shoes and gloves—to pull back their eyelids. Examinations by buttonhook were extremely painful to endure, however, and many immigrants became upset when their children or other loved ones were subjected to this treatment.

After immigrants passed through all of the medical exams, they were interviewed by inspectors who recorded all their answers in massive ledgers. These ledgers thus became the primary records of the nation's greatest age of immigration. Aided by interpreters when necessary, each immigrant answered basic questions from the inspector about age, gender, marital status, and occupation. But individuals were also asked whether they had relatives already living in America, whether they had ever been imprisoned, whether they had ever relied on public aid, and how much money they had with them.

Interviewers also asked questions designed to determine whether the applicant should be turned away on other grounds. Targets for rejection included applicants with certain religious beliefs (polygamists were barred from entering after 1891) and people with physical or mental disabilities (refused entry after 1882). Other interview questions were designed to determine whether the immigrant sitting before the inspector was likely to become a troublemaker or dependent on public aid if permitted to enter the United States. In 1891, in fact, Congress passed a law stating that any immigrant who became reliant on public welfare "within one year after his arrival" was in violation of U.S. immigration law. Such individuals were subject to immediate deportation back to their country of origin.

Another type of immigrant whose bid for entry could be rejected was the "contract" laborer—an individual who already had employment lined up prior to arrival. Immigrant contract labor was fiercely opposed by native-born American workers who viewed immigrants as a threat to their jobs, and it had been outlawed in 1885. Many people, though, noted that this law against contract labor put immigrants in a difficult position. "One provision of the Immigration Law excludes any immigrant who has no job and classifies him as likely to become a public charge, while another provision excludes an immigrant if he has a job," wrote La Guardia.

Common sense suggested that any immigrant who came into the United States in those days to settle here permanently surely came here to work. However, under the [1885] law, he could not have any more than a vague hope of a job. In answering the inspectors' questions, immigrants had to be very careful, because if their expectations were too enthusiastic, they might be held as coming in violation of the contract labor provision. Yet, if they were too indefinite, if they knew nobody, had no idea where they were going to get jobs, they might be excluded as likely to become public charges.[3]

Additional Obstacles for Women

In addition to all of these hurdles, women immigrants to America faced additional conditions for entry. Unmarried mothers and their children born out of wedlock were always turned away. Authorities feared that if these immigrants were allowed into the United States, they would become dependent on public aid—and that they would pose a risk to public morality. Married women and children without male adult escorts were only permitted to leave Ellis Island and enter the country unaccompanied by an adult male if they could prove—through a telegram, railroad tickets, or other means—that they were sponsored by American citizens or aliens who had previously established themselves in the country. These sponsors were usually relatives or fiancés.

Women were subjected to special restrictions for several reasons. First, both American and European society viewed women as intellectually inferior and thus in need of additional protection. Women also were shut out of employment in entire industries, and they were unable to command the same wages as men in those industries where they could work. As a result, officials thought that many single women, left on their own, would be lured into prostitution or become dependent on public aid in order to survive.

As a result, it was not unusual to see women at Ellis Island waiting forlornly for hours or even days to be "claimed" by a sponsor. And in some heartbreaking cases, the sponsor never came. Edward Corsi, who served as commissioner of Ellis Island in the early 1930s, wrote sympathetically about these unclaimed women:

A Hungarian woman and her daughters at Ellis Island.

There were times ... when all our efforts to locate the immediate relative failed. Sometimes a married woman had come to join her husband, or a young woman to marry her fiancée, and the man could not be located. Perhaps he had died, or moved, or the correspondence hadn't reached him—who knows? ... There was no way of soothing these heartbroken women who had traveled thousands and thousands of miles, endured suffering and humiliation, and who had uprooted their lives only to find their hopes shattered at the end of the long voyage.... If everything possible had been done, and the missing husband or fiancée still could not be traced, the poor alien, despite all her tears, had to be returned to her native country.[4]

Dreams Denied

The other immigrants who had their dreams of a new life in America crushed at Ellis Island were the 2 percent of applicants who were judged to be unacceptable risks to public health or in violation of U.S. law. Their tales of woe are the ones that were responsible for giving Ellis Island a reputation as an "Isle of Tears" among some immigrant families.

Whenever a doctor or other examiner believed that an immigrant was a candidate for deportation, he marked the immigrant's garment with a letter or symbol in chalk. Ellis Island officials used dozens of different letters and symbols to signify suspected cases of trachoma, heart problems, mental illness, and many other health concerns. Illness was the main reason that immigrants were detained, but some were also targeted for further investigation because they had no money or because they were suspected of being contract laborers, convicts, or anarchists.

Aliens who received marks on their clothes were pulled out of line and taken to special rooms for further examination. These incidents were traumatic for family groups, especially because of language barriers that sometimes left them uncertain as to why they were being separated. Even after interpreters explained the issue, families spent the next several hours or days in a terrifying limbo. They were sent to loud, crowded dormitories to anxiously await news about their loved ones. Those aliens singled out for further investigation, meanwhile, were housed in separate dormitories for men, women, and children.

Altogether, historians estimate that about 20 percent of all aliens who arrived at Ellis Island experienced some delay in their processing. The vast majority of them, however, were eventually approved. For instance, many children spent a few days in the Ellis Island hospital recovering from various illnesses—many of them contracted during the voyage from Europe—and then were reunited with their parents. Once all family members had a clean bill of health, they were allowed to go forth and begin their new lives in America.

In cases where a child's application for entrance was denied, though, the entire family suffered. These rejections were almost always for health reasons, and they destroyed the dreams of thousands of immigrant families. Since children could not travel back to Europe by themselves, a child's failure to get medical approval from authorities meant that entire families were forced to

Immigrants awaiting examination at Ellis Island.

return to their homeland. This was a cruel blow to countless families that had sold most of their worldly possessions just to buy their tickets in steerage.

Social reformers, immigration advocates, and ordinary American citizens argued that many of these scenes of heartbreak at Ellis Island could be avoided if prospective immigrants received their physical examinations before leaving Europe. These critics asserted that it made no sense to wait until the aliens reached U.S. shores before seeing if they were healthy enough to gain entrance. "Our nation is committing a gross injustice for which some day it must render an account, in allowing these hundreds of thousands of people to sell all they have, sever all connections, come four thousand miles out of the heart of Europe and other countries, only to find after passing the Statue of Liberty that they must go back to the country whence they came," declared Ellis Island Commissioner Frederick A. Wallis in 1921. "Our inspection and examination should be conducted on the other side [in Europe], thus saving thousands of people the suffering we see at this island daily which is indescribable and that would melt a heart of granite."[5]

These calls for reform went unanswered for years. But in the late 1910s and early 1920s, new laws and regulations were finally passed to address this problem. From that point forward, examinations of prospective immigrants to America were carried out in European seaports. Scenes of disappointment still occurred during these exams. But at least those who were rejected were saved from the heartbreak of being turned away from America within sight of the Statue of Liberty and the bustling streets of New York.

Managing Ellis Island

During the decades in which Ellis Island served as the primary gateway to America, the station was managed by a commissioner of immigration. The first man to hold this title was Colonel John B. Weber, who oversaw the station during its construction and first year of operation. The last man to serve as commissioner of immigration was Edward J. Shaughnessy, who was at the helm when Ellis Island closed in 1954. In between, fourteen other men held the pressure-packed job.

Two of these commissioners stand above the rest in the estimation of historians. Both William Williams and Robert Watchorn served during the early twentieth century, when the flood of immigrants from Europe reached its greatest heights. "During the peak years of immigration," observed one account, "these two men managed America's chief immigration station and coped with its complex amalgam of heartbreaking ordeals, overcrowded living conditions, and dishonest concessionaires."[6] Strangely enough, though, these two talented administrators had very different perspectives on immigration itself.

William Williams served two separate terms as commissioner, from 1902 to 1905 and again from 1909 to 1913. During his years at the helm, Williams instituted many policies and procedures that helped increase the efficiency of the island operations. He also weeded out poor employees and tore up contracts with predatory concessionaires. Time and again, he showed his dedication to making Ellis Island an effective operation that fully and impartially carried out all U.S. immigration laws.

Williams, though, personally held strong anti-immigration views. He repeatedly urged Congress to pass laws that would lessen the flow of foreigners into America. In one of his annual reports, for example, Williams wrote that immigrants from Southern and Eastern Europe "have very low standards of living, possess filthy habits, and are of an ignorance which passes belief."[7]

A Polish immigrant arriving at Ellis Island in 1907.

The strong anti-immigration views voiced by Williams made him a frequent target of attacks from pro-immigration forces in America, including foreign-language newspapers that harshly criticized him for his views.

By contrast, Robert Watchorn was a friend and ally to the immigrant. An immigrant himself, he served as commissioner during the four years (1905-

An immigrant family gazes at the Statue of Liberty from the grounds of Ellis Island.

1909) between Williams's two terms. Like Williams, Watchorn was a skilled administrator who demanded good work from the employees at Ellis Island. But Watchorn also did what he could to lessen the anxiety and discomfort of processing for new arrivals. In addition, he launched investigations of railroads and other businesses that treated immigrants unfairly. Watchorn's policies made him popular with pro-immigration groups—but extremely unpopular with the Immigration Restriction League and other forces in the United States that wanted to reduce immigration.

After the mid-1920s, the job of commissioner of immigration for Ellis Island became a much less important and visible one. During this period, inspection of migrants was moved from Ellis Island and other processing centers to the points of departure in Europe and elsewhere. In addition, new immigration laws were passed that dramatically reduced the flow of immigrants into the United States. During World War II, the number of arrivals on Ellis Island slowed to a trickle, and the island's facilities were primarily used as a detention facility for enemy aliens. Conditions did not change much after the war, and in 1954 the U.S. Immigration and Naturalization Service decided to close the facility for good.

Notes

1 Quoted in Meltzer, Milton. *Bound for America: The Story of the European Immigrants.* New York: Benchmark, 2002, p. 72.

2 La Guardia, Fiorello H. *The Making of an Insurgent: An Autobiography, 1882-1919.* Philadephia: J.B. Lippincott, 1948, p. 64.

3 La Guardia, p. 66.

4 Corsi, Edward. *In the Shadow of Liberty: The Chronicle of Ellis Island.* 1935. Reprint. New York: Arno Press, 1969, p. 80-1.

5 Quoted in Unrau, Harlan D. *Historic Resource Study (Historical Component), Vol. II, Ellis Island National Monument.* Washington DC: US Department of the Interior, 1984.

6 Chermayeff, Ivan, Fred Wasserman, and Mary J. Shapiro. *Ellis Island: An Illustrated History of the Immigrant Experience.* New York: Macmillan, 1991, p. 246.

7 Quoted in Cannato, Vincent. "Coming to America: Ellis Island and New York City." *History Now: American History Online,* March 2007. Available online at www.historynow.org/03_2007/historian2.html.

5

THE MELTING POT

◄━◄◖◗►━►

"These [immigrant] men, women, and children were, to my mind, struggling up the face of a barren precipice ... sometimes in hope, sometimes in despair, yet bitterly determined; the abyss of vice, crime, pauperism, and vagrancy was beneath them, a tiny ray of hope above them."

—Robert Hunter, *Poverty,* 1904

Once immigrants passed through Ellis Island and other processing centers across the United States, they confronted a strange and frightening world that was often far different from the one they had imagined. Many of these immigrants came from rural backgrounds, and they were overwhelmed by the sheer size of New York and other cities, as well as the chaotic clamor and bustle of American urban life. The sights, sounds, and smells of America were all unfamiliar, and many newcomers must have wondered if their newly adopted country would ever feel like home to them. "For many peasants it was the first time away from home, away from the safety of the circumscribed little villages in which they had passed all their years," observed one historian. "Now they would learn to have dealings with people essentially different from themselves. Now they would collide with unaccustomed problems, learn to understand alien ways and alien languages, manage to survive in a grossly foreign environment."[1]

City of Immigrants

More than any other American city of the late 1800s and early 1900s, New York was completely transformed by immigration. The city's labor and

61

Vibrant and crowded ethnic neighborhoods sprouted all across New York City during the great Age of Immigration.

housing patterns, its religious and political life, and its cultural flavor were all reshaped by the steady influx of individuals and families from Italy, Ireland, Russia, Austria-Hungary, Germany, Romania, Greece, and numerous other places. Of all the nation's metropolitan areas, New York City became its truest "melting pot"—a place where many different nationalities and ethnicities blended together. By the close of the nineteenth century, New York City contained 3.5 million people, more than twice as many residents as any other American city. Of this total, more than 80 percent were first- or second-generation immigrants. This influx became so great by 1900 that "in New York alone there are more persons of German descent than persons of native descent, and the German element is larger than in any city of Germany except Berlin," reported sociologist Robert Hunter. "There are nearly twice as many

Irish as in Dublin, about as many Jews as in Warsaw, and more Italians than in Naples or Venice."[2]

Some emigrants from Europe stayed in New York City because they simply had no other options. As historian Oscar Handlin wrote, "Many a new arrival who thought simply to pause in the place where he landed was entrapped and never escaped. Some had exhausted all their funds in the coming and were already paupers when they came off the ship; these were unlikely ever to earn enough to take them away. Others simply stumbled in the unsuccessful struggle to overleap the hurdles of city life."[3]

But many others who landed in New York City stayed there by choice. European Jews, for example, embraced the city. Weary of persecution in places where they were outnumbered, they settled in Jewish enclaves—neighborhoods founded by earlier generations of immigrants. And once they arrived in the United States, they rarely reconsidered their decision. For example, only one in twenty Jews who emigrated from Germany ever returned to their homeland—but more than one out of eight non-Jews eventually returned to Germany.

Jewish enclaves became larger and more prosperous as residents established a strong presence in the city's retail and garment-making trades. Within these neighborhoods, Jews could practice their faith and culture without fear. In addition, New York's multi-ethnic composition made it less likely that they would be singled out for persecution or violence when they went out into other parts of the city. One Jewish immigrant recalled that after her family emigrated from Romania in 1905 and settled in America, her mother was astounded that her daughter was treated kindly by her teacher and accepted by her fellow students. "My mother kept saying, 'It's the most wonderful thing in America that your child can go to school with gentile [non-Jewish] children, come home, her hair isn't torn, her dress isn't torn, she isn't beaten up, she comes home, walks with these children in the street....' To her, it was a miracle that nobody hit us, that nobody did anything to us."[4]

Over time, ethnic enclaves in America's great cities became principal destination points for multiple generations of immigrants. This phenomenon

> *"During the last hundred years," wrote one American immigrant, "the ever-increasing millions of natives and newcomers have poured an incalculable sum of energy and labour into the work of transforming a boundless wilderness into a garden."*

made perfect sense; why wouldn't a Hungarian or Italian or Swedish immigrant want to make his or her new home in a place where the language and customs were familiar and comforting? In fact, some ethnic neighborhoods even became further divided by regional differences in dialect and cultural practices. For example, within the "Little Italy" section of New York City—a section known for its heavy population of Italian families and Italian-owned restaurants and businesses—some streets were dominated by emigrants from Sicily and other parts of southern Italy, while other streets were composed almost exclusively of Italians from the country's northern provinces.[5]

Life in the Tenements

In many cases, though, the comfort and support provided by these communities came at the price of terrible overcrowding and deplorable living conditions. This was especially true in New York, Chicago, Philadelphia, Detroit, Pittsburgh, Cleveland, and other fast-growing industrial cities, where immigrants gathered to claim factory and construction jobs. By 1910, in fact, three out of five industrial workers in America were foreign-born.

These job opportunities put food on the table for immigrant workers, but they turned large sections of American cities into ethnic ghettos. Poorly built and maintained apartment buildings known as tenements became swollen with crowds of desperate aliens. Fire escapes and rooftops became social gathering places and even makeshift bedrooms because there simply was not enough space inside the buildings to handle all the people. City services could not keep pace with the population explosion, and streets and alleys alike became cesspools of garbage and human and animal waste. Not surprisingly, crime and disease both found fertile ground for growth in these dank and depressing areas.

Many of the individuals and families trapped in these tenements desperately wanted to leave. But many new arrivals—and even second-generation immigrants—did not have the economic power to relocate to healthier and more comfortable housing. In an age without cars or local mass transit options, workers had no other choice but to live in the shadows of the industrial factories where they worked. And competition for jobs was so fierce in many parts of the country that employers could keep wages low—even as they demanded long hours of toil in frequently dangerous working conditions. "Immigrants' livelihoods were precarious, and survival often meant that everyone in the fam-

Child employees at a cotton mill in South Carolina in 1908.

ily had to pitch in," summarized one history of the era. "After school and on weekends, youngsters helped with piecework at home or took over household chores so their mothers could go out to work. Children peddled newspapers, sold chewing gum, shined shoes, or ran errands to bring in extra income. Millions of other children joined the ranks of adult laborers and worked ten to twelve hours a day in textile mills, glass factories, canneries, and coal mines."[6]

Some Americans called on state and federal agencies to address the crushing poverty, unfair working conditions, and grim health problems that afflicted these urban pockets, but their calls went unanswered. Year after year, conditions in these "great foreign cities in our slums" worsened until they became "wildernesses of neglect," in the words of sociologist Robert Hunter.[7] Meaningful child labor and workplace safety laws were not passed until the first two decades of the twentieth century—and even then, some states were quicker to pass this type of legislation than others.

Everyone an Immigrant?

When the Industrial Revolution swept across the United States in the nineteenth century, it created new opportunities and challenges for millions of immigrants. But immigrants were not the only ones who had to navigate the turbulent waters stirred up by new technologies, new industries, and furious expansion into previously undeveloped territories. As the famous American journalist Walter Lippmann noted in his 1914 work *Drift and Mastery,* industrialization brought challenges for *all* people in America, not just newcomers. According to Lippman, the industrial era churned up feelings of unease and anxiety across all sectors of American society:

> The most dramatic revelation of this crisis is among the newer immigrants in an American city. They come suddenly from the fixed traditions of peasant life into the distracting variety of a strange civilization. America for them is not only a foreign country where they have to find a living in ways to which they are unaccustomed; America is a place where their creeds do not work, where what at home seemed big and emphatic as the mountains is almost unnoticed. It is commonplace to say that the tide of emigration [since 1890] has shifted from the Northwest to the Southeast of Europe, and that America to-day is receiving a radically different stock than it did twenty years ago. That is undoubtedly true. But the difference is not only in the immigrants. America itself is different. Those who are coming to-day have to bridge a much greater gap than did those who entered this country when it was a nation of villages.

> All of us are immigrants spiritually. We are all of us immigrants in the industrial world…. We are an uprooted people, newly arrived, and *nouveau riche* [newly rich]. As a nation we have all the vulgarity that goes with that, all the scattering of soul. The modern man is not yet settled in his world. It is strange to him, terrifying, alluring, and incomprehensibly big.

> **Source:** Lippmann, Walter. *Drift and Mastery: An Attempt to Diagnose the Current Unrest.* New York: Mitchell Kennerley, 1914, p. 208.

By the 1890s, New York City contained more than 39,000 dank and dirty tenement buildings that were stuffed with more than 1.33 million people. The vast majority of these unfortunate souls were immigrants who had fled various parts of Europe in search of a better life. Instead, some of them found themselves wishing that they had never left their homeland. "Here is a woman," explained one historian:

> In the Old Country she had lived much of her life, done most of her work, outdoors. In America, the [tenement] flat confines her. She divides up her domain by calico sheets hung on ropes, tries to make a place for her people and possessions. But there is no place and she has not room to turn about. It is true, everything is in poor repair, the rain comes through the ceilings, the wind blows dirt through the cracks in the wall. But she does not even know how to go about restoring order, establishing cleanliness. She breaks her back to exterminate the proliferating vermin. What does she get? A dozen lice behind the collar.[8]

To some observers, the conditions in the tenements indicated that the American dream of equal opportunity and good fortune would remain out of reach for entire generations of immigrants. According to their perspectives, the conditions in the tenements seemed to call into question whether America was truly a place where all men and women could meet their fullest potential, irrespective of their ethnic heritage or religious background.

In fact, Hunter and other reformers charged that native-born Americans seemed increasingly willing to lay the foundations for their own comfort and prosperity on the bruised and ragged shoulders of long-suffering immigrant laborers. "In the poorest quarters of many great American cities and industrial communities one is struck by a most peculiar fact—the poor are almost entirely foreign born," wrote Hunter.

> On a small scale we have Russia's poverty, Poland's poverty, Italy's poverty, Hungary's poverty, Bohemia's poverty—and what other nation's have we not? ... In certain large cities of this country almost everything separates "the classes and the masses" except the feeling which inheres in the word "humanity." The rich and well-to-do are mostly Americans; the poor

are mostly foreign, drawn from among the miserable of every nation. The citizen and the slave of Greece were scarcely more effectually separated.... In [other] countries there are the masters and the workmen; the rich and the poor, separated by wealth, by position, and by place of dwelling. But in the largest cities of America there are many other things which separate the rich and the poor. Language, institutions, customs, and even religion separate the native and the foreigner. It is this separation which makes the problem of poverty in America more difficult of solution than that of any other nation.[9]

Despite all this, however, many of the immigrants who toiled in the factories, mills, oil fields, and smelters of turn-of-the-century America continued to persevere. They refused to give up, even as disease, crime, workplace accidents, and feelings of hopelessness picked off fellow immigrants to their left and right. And for millions of these men and women, the years of hard work eventually enabled them to build better lives for their families—and a proud legacy to pass on to their children.

Looking Beyond the Cities

From its opening in 1892 until its closure in 1954, Ellis Island processed the arrival of twelve million immigrants to America's shores. About four million of these aliens settled in the New York metropolitan area, but the remaining eight million built lives in other parts of the country. Industrial cities in the Northeast and the Great Lakes region were the leading destination for these immigrants, but the territories of the Great Plains, the Southwest, and the West Coast also received significant immigrant infusions. The Deep South, on the other hand, received comparatively few immigrants during this period. Economic opportunities were more limited in the South than in other parts of the country, and immigrants distrusted its history of racial violence and bigotry.

Unlike some of the industrial cities of the North, which struggled mightily to absorb the relentless waves of new immigrants, less populated parts of the West were eager to accept newcomers. Business leaders and legislators west of the Mississippi River actively campaigned to attract the attention of immigrants, which were seen as key to the settlement and economic development of the West. And over time, their efforts to lure immigrants away from the great cities of the East gained momentum.

Immigrants wait to board a train in Minneapolis, c. 1910.

America's all-powerful railroad industry played a central role in these campaigns. The Iron Horse, as the locomotive was often called, completely reshaped the economic and societal character of the United States during the nineteenth century. This exciting technology made it much easier for manufacturers and farmers to send their products to market, allowed harvesters of coal, timber, and other natural resources to penetrate the most remote corners of the continent, and made coast-to-coast travel a practical reality for the first time. Railroad promoter and land speculator William Gilpin spoke for millions of nineteenth-century Americans when he declared that "railways, multiplied and spanning the continent, are essential domestic institutions—more powerful and more permanent than law, or popular consent, or political constitutions. They thoroughly complete the grand system ... which fraternizes us into one people."[10]

Once railroads came to be accepted as essential to the settlement of the West and the economic development of the entire nation, the federal government worked mightily to aid the industry. During the 1850s, 1860s, and 1870s the federal government gave huge land grants to the railroads. All told, dozens of railroads received grants of western land totaling more than 170 million acres during this time. As soon as they received these gifts, railroad companies turned their attention to convincing immigrants and restless native-born citizens of the East to come settle it. The railroad owners knew that if they could bring farmers, miners, ranchers, craftsmen, and storekeepers to their empty lands, their landholdings would jump in value. Even more importantly, they would be able to generate increased revenue from transporting wheat, corn, coal, timber, cattle, and other trade goods produced by these settlers.

Selling the West

Determined to maximize their profits, American railroads became the single greatest voice urging new immigrants to consider starting their new lives in the West. They set up sophisticated operations in major eastern port cities to convince new arrivals from Europe to look west for their fortunes. Promoters distributed colorful posters, brochures, and pamphlets throughout ethnic neighborhoods. These pieces of propaganda described wide swaths of the West as wonderlands of natural beauty, rich farming soil, and ideal weather.

Some of these promotional brochures provided a fairly accurate reflection of conditions in California and other parts of the West. Some regions *did* have good weather, good soil, and abundant resources. As a result, from the 1850s through the 1880s, "immigrants and disenchanted easterners poured into prairie states like Nebraska, Iowa, and Missouri, their imaginations alight with the promises of prosperity fed to them by the railroad land agents who prowled the streets of New York, Boston, and Philadelphia."[11] Many of these fortune seekers left for the West via special "immigrant trains" that the railroad companies established in the nation's leading eastern seaports.

Other promotional campaigns, though, used blatant falsehoods to lure immigrants. Railroad companies that operated in semi-arid territories of the Great Plains, for example, brazenly misled settlers about soil quality and rainfall levels. In many cases, these claims worked just as well as the more legitimate ones.

American railroad companies devoted even more energy to their promotional efforts in Europe. Their widely distributed posters, pamphlets, and other advertisements, combined with those of steamship companies and others who benefited financially from immigration, exerted a powerful pull on

Finnish-American loggers pose at a Great Lakes timber camp, c. 1915.

millions of restless Europeans. U.S. railroad giants sold hundreds of thousands of tickets each year to European immigrants. Many of these tickets were package deals that included steamship passage to Ellis Island or other major points of entry.

One of the most successful strategies employed by the railroads was to encourage "group settlement" or colonization. Under these plans, large groups of families from a single European village or town agreed to relocate to the American West and re-establish their community there. These arrangements were enormously profitable to railroads because it enabled them to sell dozens or even hundreds of tickets at one time. But colonization provided genuine benefits to immigrants as well. It enabled them to resettle in America among familiar neighbors who held the same values, beliefs, cultural traditions, and farming practices—and spoke the same language. As a result, group settlement was promoted by a wide range of religious groups and benevolent societies in Europe as a way to simultaneously maintain Old World beliefs and enjoy New World prosperity.

Ethnic Germans from Russia, Swedish Lutherans, and Irish Catholics were among the leaders of the colonization method of immigration. These and other groups transplanted themselves all the way from Europe to various parts of the Midwest, Great Plains, and Intermountain West. Once they reached their destinations, they dusted off their cultural traditions and religious practices at the same time that they unpacked their clothing, family heirlooms, and farming tools.

Sometimes these mass relocations from Europe were initiated by a single individual or family who became established, then sent word back home for others to follow. These so-called migration chains became an important element in the settlement of the West. By 1900, in fact, "the majority of immigrants were traveling on prepaid tickets sent from America, indicating the remarkable strength of family ties and the human desire for roots and continuity."[12]

However they arrived in the West, the new immigrants immediately lent their labor and ingenuity and determination to the cause of settlement and development. And their contributions, combined with the efforts of native-born Americans, transformed the continent into a mighty economic machine that generated ever-greater percentages of the planet's production of wheat, cotton, oil, beef, and other goods. This knowledge was a source of tremendous pride for immigrants such as British-born Horace J. Bridges. Writing in his 1919 memoir *On Becoming an American,* Bridges declared that

> During the last hundred years, the ever-increasing millions of natives and newcomers have poured an incalculable sum of energy and labour into the work of transforming a boundless wilderness into a garden. Nothing in the world's history is comparable with what has been done here. We have million-peopled cities where, within the memory of men yet living, there were primeval solitudes. Trackless deserts and virgin mountains have been spanned by magnificent railways. What has elsewhere been the growth of generations and centuries has here been accomplished in years and decades.[13]

Finding Work

Wherever immigrants decided to settle in America, their first priority was to find jobs. In many cases, ethnic groups were drawn to regions where the dominant industries could make use of skills and knowledge that the immigrants already possessed. In other words, immigrants who had worked as farmers, miners, and textile-makers in Europe gravitated to regions of the United States where farming, mining, and textile jobs could be found. By the late 1800s, this phenomenon was evident all around the country. "Many Scandinavians traveled to Minnesota and went into farming, while Slavic groups tended to go to the mines and steel mills in Pennsylvania and slaughterhouses in Chicago," explained one history of the era. "French Canadians made up the majority of workers in New England's textile mills. Mexicans, Japanese, Chinese and Filipinos generally headed for California and other western states, where they worked in farming and manufacturing or opened small businesses.... By 1897, about 75 percent of the construction workers in New York City were Italian immigrants, and the same was true of other major cities."[14]

This tremendous influx of immigrant labor received a mixed reception in America. Certainly, the owners and managers of the country's factories, mills, construction companies, and shipyards were happy to receive these workers. The immigrants provided them with a vast pool of labor willing to work long hours in poor conditions for meager pay. As a famous 1907-1908 report by the Russell Sage Foundation bluntly stated, the powerful Pittsburgh-based Carnegie Steel empire liked to hire new immigrants because of "their habit of silent submission ... and their willingness to work long hours and overtime without a murmur."[15]

These same attributes, however, greatly alarmed workers who were already struggling to make ends meet in America. The leadership of early labor unions such as the American Federation of Labor and the Knights of Labor opposed unrestricted immigration as a threat to good wages and job security. These groups played an important role in the passage of laws such as one in 1885 that outlawed "contract laborers"—immigrants who came to America with jobs already promised to them. And their hostility to immigrants became even greater after factory owners began using immigrants as strike breakers—workers called in to replace employees who called labor strikes to seek better wages and working conditions.

The labor movement of the late nineteenth and early twentieth centuries, though, was not unified on this issue. Some workers believed that immigrants who were brought into the union fold could actually increase labor's power and leverage in its dealings with management. And they argued that bigotry against the new wave of immigrants was not only unwise but unjust. "We have no right to raise a cry against any class of human beings because of their nationality," declared the Irish-born union activist Joseph McDonnell.

> Let our first stand be against those rich and intelligent thieves who strive to perpetuate and establish a system of overwork and starvation pay. And then against all those, whether they be Chinese or American, Irish or English, French or German, Spanish or Italian who refuse to cooperate with us for their good and ours, and that of the whole human family.... We favor every effort against the conspiracy of the rich to import cheap labor from Europe and Asia, but we warn the working-men that no action but International Labor action, and no cry but that of high wages and short hours will lead us into the promised land of peace, plenty, and happiness.[16]

But cultural and language barriers, combined in some cases with long-standing ethnic tensions between different groups, made unionizing the immigrants a difficult task. In addition, many companies and industries actively worked to stoke ethnic tensions between different groups so as to keep them from taking united stands against management.

Helping Hands and Cold Shoulders

Immigrants also received a mixed reception from the wider American public. Some native-born Americans and long-established emigrants from Western Europe saw no reason to fear the men and women who poured into the United States from Eastern Europe, Asia, and elsewhere during the late 1800s and early 1900s. They did not view the arrival of these newcomers as a threat to American culture and vitality. Instead, they saw their entrance as an opportunity for national enrichment. They also recognized that many immigrants were eager to assimilate and become fully "American" (see "Forging a New Identity in America," p. 172).

Finally, immigration supporters believed that by taking the best elements of each ethnic group, America could forge a new and exciting identity for itself. And many of these Americans believed that they had a moral obligation to lend a helping hand to the newcomers. "Everybody had something to give

Some Italian immigrants supported themselves in America as fruit vendors, selling their wares at open-air markets.

me for help," recalled a Jew who emigrated from Russia in 1908. "It wasn't a question of money, it was a question of being a human being to a human being. And in those days people were apparently that way. There were so many nice people that were trying to help us when we came to this country."[17]

Support for immigrants took many other forms as well. Influential journalists like Jacob Riis sought to assure fellow Americans that schools and other institutions would help newcomers assimilate. "While the [American] flag flies over the public school, keep it aloft over Ellis Island and have no misgivings. The school has the answer to your riddle."[18] This confidence proved well-placed. American schools taught young immigrants how to read, write, and speak English and instructed them in U.S. history, government, and customs. In numerous instances, this deep indoctrination into the national culture helped children become "American" much more quickly than their parents.

Immigrant children playing on the roof of an elementary school in Boston in 1909.

In addition, social reformers like Jane Addams, Lillian Wald, and Grace Abbott founded influential charitable organizations and settlement houses to help immigrant families survive in the big cities. By 1910, more than 400 settlement houses across the country were providing a helping hand to newcomers. These facilities assisted immigrants with everything from finding jobs and providing child care to learning English. Settlement houses also became important rallying places for urban reformers seeking to improve workplace safety, eliminate child labor, and strengthen municipal trash collection, tenement inspections, and public aid programs. Their efforts bore fruit in the first two decades of the twentieth century, when many laws designed to protect workers and consumers—and rein in the power and greed of corporations—were passed at local, state, and federal levels.

Another important source of aid for new immigrants was the benevolent society. These groups were charitable organizations established by various ethnic and religious groups to help needy fellow members when they came to America. For example, New York City's Russian Jews formed the Hebrew Immigrant Aid Society (HIAS) to provide shelter, meals, transportation, and job leads for fellow Jews after they landed at Ellis Island. The HIAS even provided legal defense services for Jews who were targeted for deportation by Ellis Island inspectors. "Immigrants used to come in crying and crying," recalled one Jewish immigrant who eventually took a job with HIAS. "My heart would break, and naturally you tried to do the best you could for them. Having been an immigrant, I knew what they're going through."[19]

Other segments of American society, however, did not welcome the immigrants that poured into the country from the 1870s through the early 1920s (see "A Native-born American Lashes Out at East European Immigrants," p. 152). In addition to the opposition based on fears about job security and wages, many Americans simply believed that the newcomers posed a threat to their way of life. Some believed that America's unity and strength would gradually fade if it was forever trying to assimilate different ethnic traditions and belief systems. Concerns were also raised about the fast-dwindling availability of public land for settlement and development, as well as America's depletion of its forests and other natural resources.

Others opposed immigration for more nakedly bigoted reasons. They thought that the new immigrants hailing from southern and eastern Europe and Asia were of inferior moral character and intelligence, and they treated them with the same contempt that they directed at Native Americans and African Americans whose distant ancestors had been born on American soil. "They wanted the complete exclusion of people different from themselves," wrote Progessive Era historian Michael McGerr. "Not content to let immigrants live apart in urban enclaves, these Americans ... advocated immigration restriction, a wall built around the United States."[20] And in 1924, after nearly a half-century of effort, these anti-immigration forces finally got what they wanted.

Notes

[1] Handlin, Oscar. *The Uprooted.* 1951. Reprint. Philadelphia: University of Pennsylvania Press, 2002, p. 35.

[2] Hunter, Robert. *Poverty.* New York: Macmillan, 1904, p. 262.

[3] Handlin, p. 49.

[4] Quoted in Coan, Peter Morton. *Ellis Island Interviews: In Their Own Words.* New York: Facts on File, 1997, p. 328.

[5] *Immigrants: The New Americans.* Editors of Time-Life Books. New York: Time-Life, 1999, p. 49.

[6] Chermayeff, Ivan, Fred Wasserman, and Mary J. Shapiro. *Ellis Island: An Illustrated History of the Immigrant Experience.* New York: Macmillan, 1991, pp. 63-64.

[7] Hunter, p. 266.

[8] Handlin, pp. 135-6.

[9] Hunter, pp. 262-63.

[10] Quoted in *New Perspectives on the West,* PBS, 1996. Available online at www.pbs.org/thewest/program/episodes/five/onepeople.htm

[11] Hillstrom, Kevin. "Origins and Development," in *The Industrial Revolution in America: Railroads.* Edited by Kevin Hillstrom and Laurie Collier Hillstrom. Santa Barbara, CA: ABC-CLIO, 2005, p. 22.

[12] Chermayeff, p. 26.

[13] Bridges, Horace J. *On Becoming an American: Some Meditations of a Newly Naturalized Immigrant.* Boston: M. Jones, 1919, p. 10.

[14] Chermayeff, p. 56, 59.

[15] Fitch, John. *The Pittsburgh Survey, Vol. 3: The Steel Workers.* New York: Charities Publication Committee, 1910.

[16] McDonnell, Joseph. "The Chinese Must Go." *Labor Standard* (New York), June 30, 1878. Available online at www.digitalhistory.uh.edu/asian_voices/voices_display.cfm?id=24.

[17] Quoted in Chermayeff, p. 76.

[18] McGerr, Michael. *A Fierce Discontent: The Rise and Fall of the Progressive Movement in America.* New York: Oxford University Press, 2003, p. 211.

[19] Quoted in Coan, p. 245.

[20] McGerr, p. 211.

6

SHUTTING THE GOLDEN DOOR

The American people have come to sanction—indeed demand—reform of our immigration laws. They have seen, patent and plain, the encroachments of the foreign-born flood upon their own lives.... The day of indiscriminate acceptance of all races has definitely ended.

—Albert Johnson, leading author
of the Immigration Act of 1924

Even as far back as colonial days, Americans debated the wisdom of unrestricted immigration. Few workers expressed fear that new immigrants would depress wages or take their jobs during this era. But many lashed out against any immigrant who was not a member of their own ethnic "tribe." They distrusted immigrants who held social and religious customs that were different from their own. Critics openly worried that mass waves of immigration from nations other than England would weaken America. Even some of the nation's greatest historical figures harbored such views at one time or another in their careers. The legendary Benjamin Franklin, for example, openly condemned the arrival of immigrants from places other than England (see "Benjamin Franklin Attacks Immigration," p. 81).

Despite such sentiments, however, the United States resisted placing any legal restrictions on immigration during its first hundred years of existence. Congress did pass the Alien and Sedition Acts of 1798, which imposed some limits on residency and gave federal authorities new powers to deport "undesirable" aliens. But these acts were aimed at defending the nation from radical agitators rather than curbing immigration, and many Americans thought that they were unconstitutional. When Thomas Jefferson became president in early 1801, he pardoned everyone who had been convicted under the Acts. By 1802 the laws had been repealed or allowed to expire.

After this controversy faded, the United States did not pass any federal laws or guidelines on immigration until the early 1880s. "As a general matter," explained one historical work, "no one really cared how many newcomers came to the United States, since there was plenty of land and work for everyone."[1]

The Know-Nothings

The only major interruption to this eighty-year period of peaceful immigration came in the 1850s. During that time, a group that came to be known as the "Know-Nothings" arose in response to the massive waves of Irish Catholic immigrants fleeing poverty and famine in their native country.

The Know-Nothings viewed the Irish newcomers as uncivilized, brutish, and immoral creatures who were blindly loyal to the Pope. Its members warned that the Irish posed a threat to America's Protestant heritage, and they stirred up anti-Irish feelings in cities and rural hamlets alike. In town after town, businesses posted signs informing Irish people that they were not welcome as employees or customers.

The official name of the Know-Nothings was the Order of the Star-Spangled Banner. This secret organization earned its more common name, though, from instructions it gave to all members to state that they "know nothing" when asked about the Order. Only Protestant men who had been born on U.S. soil were eligible. Members also had to take an oath supporting the Order's opposition to Catholicism and its demand that all public offices be held by native-born Protestants.

By the mid-1850s, the Know-Nothings viewed the growing Irish ghettos in New York, Boston, and other eastern cities as proof that the newcomers were unfit for American citizenship—even though the hatred they fanned was a major factor in the Irish immigrants' struggle to escape poverty. They blamed the Irish and other non-Protestant immigrants for virtually every problem confronting the nation, from labor unrest to rising levels of crime in the cities. Conveniently, their demonization of the Irish allowed native-born Americans to avoid taking any responsibility for any of these complex trends.

Benjamin Franklin Attacks Immigration

Benjamin Franklin is one of America's most famous Founding Fathers, but he also issued some of the earliest public calls for limits on immigration. In his 1751 work *Observations Concerning the Increase of Mankind,* Franklin expressed extreme unhappiness with the growing number of German immigrants in Pennsylvania. "Why should Pennsylvania, founded by the English, become a Colony of *Aliens,* who will shortly be so numerous as to Germanize us instead of us Anglifying them, and will never adopt our Language or Customs, any more than they can acquire our Complexion," he wrote.

Elsewhere in *Observations,* Franklin proposed an immigration policy for the colonies that was explicitly racist. "Why Increase the Sons of Africa, by Planting them in America, where we have so fair an Opportunity, by excluding all Blacks and Tawneys, of increasing the lovely White and Red?" he declared.

In later years, though, Franklin did not repeat these proposals. Instead, he expressed greater appreciation for the bravery and fortitude of all men and women who came to build new lives in America. By his later years, Franklin had abandoned his youthful nativism and become a supporter of European immigration to the United States.

Sources: Isaacson, Walter. *Benjamin Franklin: An American Life.* New York: Simon and Schuster, 2003.

Leonard W. Labaree, ed. *The Papers of Benjamin Franklin.* New Haven, CT: Yale University Press, 1961.

For a few short years, the Know-Nothings appeared poised to transform American life and politics for generations to come. The group boasted a membership of almost one million white men—a huge number of potential voters in the still-young nation. It also fielded or supported anti-immigration candidates that took office all across the country. In 1854-1855 alone, anti-immigration candidates took more than 100 seats in the U.S. Congress, claimed the governorships of eight states, and won the mayor's office in Boston, Chicago, and Philadelphia.[2]

Excited by these triumphs, the Order hammered together a set of national anti-immigration goals that included extending the residency requirements for gaining naturalized citizen status from five to twenty-one years. The group's leadership also supported a constitutional amendment that would bar foreign-born or Catholic citizens from holding *any* public office, as well as new laws to severely limit annual immigration numbers.

"Where would your mines have been dug and worked, where would your great iron industries and constructions … have been were it not for the immigrants?" demanded one pro-immigration lawmaker.

In 1856 the Order formed a new political party called the American Party and recruited ex-president Millard Fillmore as its presidential candidate. Fillmore managed to get about 22 percent of the popular vote in the 1856 election by running on an "Americans must rule America" platform. But strong opposition from first- and second-generation Americans put him far behind Republican candidate John Fremont (33 percent) and Democratic winner James Buchanan (45 percent).

Fillmore's distant third-place finish took a huge toll on the morale of the Know-Nothings, and the group never recovered. By 1860 the Order had completely collapsed. One year later the Civil War erupted. Immigrants played such a huge role in both the Union and Confederate armies during this conflict that anti-immigrant voices could find little public support for their positions when the war finally ended. In 1868, in fact, the United States adopted the Fourteenth Amendment, which expanded citizenship to include the nation's vast population of freed African-American slaves.

The Federal Government Takes Control

After the Civil War, though, even many of America's staunchest defenders of immigration were forced to admit that something had to be done to impose some order on the immigration process. Every year, hundreds of thousands of newcomers were pouring into America, but no effective system existed for identifying these immigrants, rejecting criminals and disease-carriers in their midst, and helping the rest to avoid the swindlers and thieves waiting to prey on them.

A few cities had tried to do this job themselves, but they had been overwhelmed. In 1824, for example, New York City imposed rules requiring immigrant ships to provide state agents with manifests that listed each passenger's name, birth date, occupation, and physical condition. Other efforts followed, including the city's establishment of the Castle Garden immigrant processing station in 1855. But these measures failed to bring order to the immigration process, and by the 1870s there was a growing feeling that the federal government needed to step in. Advocates of federal intervention believed that national immigration laws and regulations could harness this incoming flood of workers and settlers in ways that would most benefit the fast-growing American nation.

Unfortunately, the first major action that Congress took to regulate immigration into the United States was to pass one of the most racist pieces of legislation in American history. The Chinese Exclusion Act of 1882 was rooted in American fears and ignorance about the so-called Yellow Peril—a belief that Chinese immigrants, who looked and dressed differently from whites and had non-Christian religious beliefs, might destroy the nation's cultural and political foundations if they were not stopped.

Much of the anti-Chinese hysteria was based in the American West, where most Chinese immigrants were located. White workers viewed them as a dangerous threat to their own jobs and wages, in part because Chinese laborers were known up and down the West Coast as tireless workers who were willing to accept extremely low pay. These white fears became even greater after the 1869 completion of the Transcontinental Railroad threw thousands of Chinese laborers out of work (see "Chinese Invasion," p. 145). Republican senator George Henry Williams of Oregon darkly warned that if Chinese immigration was not halted, "millions of heathens and pagans [would eventually gain the] power to control our institutions."[3]

Other Americans rose up in defense of Chinese immigration (see "A Defense of Chinese Immigrants in America," p. 148). "If the Chinese come here, they will come for citizenship or merely for labor," argued Republican Senator Charles Sumner of Massachusetts, who had gained fame prior to the Civil War for his strong abolitionist beliefs. "If they come for citizenship, then in this desire do they give a pledge of loyalty to our institutions; and where is the peril in such vows?"[4]

But Sumner and his allies could not hold back the anti-Chinese momentum. The Chinese Exclusion Act was passed by Congress and signed into law by President Chester A. Arthur. This law banned virtually all Chinese immi-

This vicious anti-Chinese lithograph portrays Chinese workers as willing to live in crowded opium dens and eat rats for survival, comparing them unfavorably to upstanding white workers.

gration for ten years and forbade U.S. courts from granting citizenship to Chinese already living in the United States. The law was later renewed in 1892 and 1902, and it was not repealed until 1943.

Other immigration restrictions were passed in the 1880s and early 1890s, including an 1885 law that turned away "contract laborers"—prospective immigrants who already had jobs lined up in the United States. The Immigration Act of 1891, meanwhile, created the office of Superintendent of Immigration within the Treasury Department to oversee all immigration issues (in 1903 the Immigration Service was transferred to the Department of Commerce and Labor, and in 1940 it came under the jurisdiction of the Department of Justice).

The 1891 Act also required all aliens entering the United States to submit to inspections to determine whether they would be allowed to step on

American soil. One year later, the Ellis Island immigration station opened in New York Harbor. Since New York had major transatlantic connections to Europe, the Ellis Island facility immediately became the main locale where U.S. immigration laws were carried out.

New Calls for Immigration Restrictions

Even as Ellis Island was opening its doors, anti-immigrant sentiments became more apparent in many parts of America. This resurgence in hostility was driven by rising worker-management tensions, growing alarm about ethnic slums in U.S. cities, and a pronounced rise in immigration from southeastern Europe. The latter development greatly disturbed many Americans whose ancestors had lived in England, Germany, and other parts of northeastern Europe. Much of America's culture reflected their own cultural background, and they did not want Italians, Greeks, Hungarians, Slavs, and other unfamiliar ethnic groups to change it in any way.

These fears were heightened by some influential voices. Terence V. Powderly, who served as Commissioner of Immigration from 1897 to 1902, issued repeated calls for new immigration restrictions. A former leader of the Knights of Labor union, Powderly saw unrestricted immigration as a dire threat to American craftsmen and laborers. The only groups who escaped his wrath were British, German, and Scandinavian immigrants, whom he thought could enter America without causing undue disruption.[5]

William Williams, who served two four-year terms as Ellis Island commissioner in the early 1900s, also called for new restrictions. He argued that immigrants had no inherent right to enter the United States, and that the nation's future prosperity hinged on keeping out "those who are below a certain grade of intellectual and economic fitness." Williams further declared that "it is almost certain that had our early immigration proceeded from these portions of Eastern and Southern Europe which are now sending such large numbers of illiterate aliens into our great cities, this country would not now enjoy its present civilization."[6]

Newspaper and magazine publishers and editors also played a big role in stoking the growing anti-immigrant fervor. Newspapers and magazines were the primary source of news and information for Americans at the turn of the century, and some of them described the new waves of immigrants as immoral brutes or lunatics. Others charged that unrestricted immigration

Massachusetts Senator Henry Cabot Lodge was the chief legislative ally of the Immigration Restriction League.

was turning the United States into "The World's Dumping Ground."[7] These arguments were also carried forward by influential writers like Josiah Strong, who grimly stated in his 1891 book *Our Country: Its Possible Future and Its Present Crisis* that "the typical immigrant is a European peasant, whose horizon has been narrow, whose moral and religious training has been meager or false, and whose ideas of life are low."[8]

The Immigration Restriction League

The most influential anti-immigration voice of this era, though, was the Immigration Restriction League. This group was founded in 1894 by a powerful group of Bostonians who opposed the growing influence of Irish Americans in the political and economic life of the region. The two leading figures in the group were Prescott F. Hall and Republican Congressman Henry Cabot Lodge of Massachusetts.

Rather than fight for outright quotas on the number of immigrants permitted to enter the United States each year, Hall and Lodge came up with a different strategy. They called for a literacy test for all prospective immigrants. Under this proposal, alien applicants who were unable to prove that they could read and write fluently in their native language would be barred from entering the country.

Over the next several years, the Immigration Restriction League nearly succeeded in passing legislation that would have enshrined the literacy test in U.S. immigration law. In 1897 a literacy bill passed both houses of Congress, but it was vetoed by President Grover Cleveland two days before he left office. "It is infinitely more safe to admit a hundred thousand immigrants who, though unable to read and write, seek among us only a home and an opportunity to work," declared Cleveland, "than to admit one of those unruly agitators and enemies of governmental control who can not only read and write, but delights in arousing by unruly speech the illiterate and peacefully minded to discontent and tumult."[9]

Political Tightrope

Some American lawmakers condemned the strengthening anti-immigrant tide. New York Congressman Samuel McMillan, for example, angrily attacked supporters of the literacy test. "Where would your mines have been dug and worked, where would your great iron industries and constructions ... have been were it not for the immigrants?" he stated. "It is the immigrant that bears the burden of hard labor ... and has contributed his full share to the building up of our great country."[10]

But Lodge and his allies in Congress refused to give up, and the whole literacy test issue became a difficult political challenge for the men who occupied the White House in the early twentieth century. Even President Theodore Roosevelt, who took great pleasure in political battle, seemed uncertain how to address the issue during his presidency (1901-1909). On the one hand, Roosevelt recognized industry's need for workers and had a high regard for honest and hardworking immigrants. On the other hand, he believed that immigrants were responsible for some of the nation's social unrest. In addition, Roosevelt held some personal prejudices against people from ethnic backgrounds different than his own.

Roosevelt's clearest declaration on the subject did not come until he left office. "There is no room in this country for hyphenated Americanism," Roosevelt declared in a rebuke to immigrants and native-born Americans who described themselves as Irish-Americans, Italian-Americans, Polish-Americans, and so forth. "We must unsparingly condemn any man who holds any other allegiance. But if he is heartily and singly loyal to this Republic, then no matter where he was born, he is just as good an American as anyone else."[11]

Even some observers who were sympathetic to the challenges faced by new immigrants in America weighed in on the side of the anti-immigration forces. In his 1904 book *Poverty,* Robert Hunter wrote at length about the bravery and fortitude of poor immigrants in America's urban slums. But he also asserted that "it seems unquestionable that the unfittest class of immigrants that have ever come to our shores is increasing yearly in numbers. We may and should be willing to permit our native stock to be annihilated by a

This 1916 political cartoon depicts Uncle Sam standing behind a high "Literacy Test" wall spiked with pen points and telling an immigrant family that "You're welcome in—if you can climb it."

superior people but it is inconceivable that we should knowingly promote, by conscious act, an intermarrying and intermingling of peoples, which will indefinitely lower the standard of American or any other manhood."[12]

By the early 1910s, a literacy test for immigrants was once again being seriously considered by Congress. The idea received another boost in support in 1910 and 1911, when a joint House of Representatives-Senate committee called the Dillingham Commission—which included Lodge—issued a scathing series of reports blaming many of America's social and economic problems on emigrants from southern and eastern Europe. The Commission concluded that emigration from these regions should be greatly reduced—and it identified a "reading and writing test as the most feasible single method of restricting undesirable immigration."[13]

The Battle Rages On

After the Dillingham Commission's 41-volume report was released, the battle between pro- and anti-immigration forces reached new heights. On the pro-immigration side, legislators such as James Michael Curley—an Irish-American who served as a U.S. Congressman, mayor of Boston, and governor of Massachusetts during his distinguished career—described the literacy test as inherently "un-American."

Other opponents insisted that the literacy test showed no recognition of the horrible conditions in which many immigrants from southeastern Europe had grown up. "Where will these people who have been robbed of their country go if you shall enact this illiteracy test?" asked N.L. Piotrowski, a Polish-American businessman from Chicago, during one immigration hearing in Washington. He noted that education was not supported or funded by the rulers of his native land. "For that reason about 38 percent or 40 percent of these people have no chance to obtain any education," he said. "If the illiteracy test were a test of good character ... I would not object to it. But it is not a good test of character; it is not a good test of the real worth of men."[14]

Anti-immigration forces, though, countered with their own arguments. "An immigrant who can read furnishes better material, all things considered, for the building up of the American people, than one who cannot," insisted the Immigration Restriction League. "Assimilation is an intellectual process, accomplished with the greatest difficulty in the lifetime of any adult immi-

Flu Epidemic Fuels Anti-German Bigotry

When the United States entered World War I in 1917 to fight Germany, many Americans of German backgrounds faced heightened levels of prejudice and distrust from their fellow countrymen. This fear of German traitors in their midst was fed by some politicians and newspaper editors. Some of these individuals genuinely believed that a threat existed. Others used public fear to boost domestic support for the war effort. In the wake of this hostility, many U.S. churches and fraternal organizations founded by German immigrants suffered vandalism, violence, and intimidation. Other immigrants felt the sting of renewed discrimination as well, and they were not helped when President Woodrow Wilson accused "hyphenated Americans" of dumping the "poison of disloyalty into the very arteries of our national life."

Anti-German hysteria reached even greater heights across America in late 1918, when a Spanish flu epidemic swept across the globe. This horrible flu struck terror into the hearts of people everywhere. It killed an estimated 675,000 people in the United States alone, and claimed as many as 40 million lives worldwide before it ran its course in the second half of 1919.

Many Americans believed that the flu originated as a biological warfare attack from Germany. They knew that chemical weapons were being used in the war in Europe, and wartime fervor provided a fertile environment for the spreading of such rumors. Even some of the nation's most respected newspapers believed the rumors to be true. "Let the curse [of the flu] be called the German plague," fumed the *New York Times* in October 1918. "Let every child learn to associate what is accursed with the word German not in the spirit of hate but in the spirit of contempt born of the hateful truth which Germany has proved herself to be." As this false rumor spread like wildfire in taverns, factory floors, and living rooms across the country, countless innocent German-Americans were shunned or harassed. And long after the epidemic ended and the war concluded, German immigrants found it difficult to gain acceptance in many parts of the country.

Source: Kreiser, Christine M. "The Enemy Within." *American History,* Dec. 2006.

grant, and quite impossible in the case of an immigrant whose early environment and social traditions have been widely diverse from our own."[15]

Many opponents of immigration also rolled out "scientific evidence" that some races were just naturally superior to others in terms of their potential for mental, physical, and moral advancement. One of the most influential men to advance these now-discredited theories was Madison Grant, a leader of the Immigration Restriction League who also expressed horror at any sexual activity between races. "What is the greatest danger which threatens the American republic to-day?" he asked in his popular 1916 book *The Passing of the Great Race*. "I would certainly reply: The gradual dying out among our people of these hereditary traits through which the principles of our religious, political, and social foundation were laid down, and their insidious replacement by traits of less noble character."[16]

The Gate Begins to Swing Shut

In 1913 President William Howard Taft vetoed a version of the literacy test. Two years later, President Woodrow Wilson followed suit. But still the pressure continued, and in 1916 Congress passed the Federal Immigration Act. Wilson vetoed this legislation as well, but in early 1917 Congress overrode the president's veto by an overwhelming majority to make it law.

This act put major new restrictions on immigration. It expanded those immigrants banned from entering the country to include "idiots," "feebleminded persons," and any other applicants found to be "mentally or physically defective." It also established an "Asiatic Barred Zone" that excluded most Asians—not just Chinese—from being admitted into the country. Finally, it included the long-demanded literacy test. Under this legislation, every immigrant over the age of fourteen had to be able to read in their native language.

At first, the new law did not have that great an impact. The eruption of World War I in 1914 had choked off most shipping across the Atlantic, so many prospective emigrants from Europe had no way to reach the United States anyway. But when the war ended in 1918, the full impact of the law was immediately felt. The new literacy requirements proved to be a heavy burden for many immigrants who hailed from countries with poor education systems or cultures that were heavily reliant on spoken word and oral traditions.

Still, anti-immigrant forces were not satisfied with the passage of the Federal Immigration Act. They continued to press for even greater restric-

Ku Klux Klan chapters such as this one on parade in Washington, DC, in the early 1920s focused much of their hatred on immigrants after World War I.

tions, often employing arguments that displayed their unapologetic hatred for peoples different from themselves.

In 1924, for example, South Carolina Senator Ellison DuRant Smith drew on Grant's theories to call for a complete end to immigration. "I think we now have sufficient population in our country for us to shut the door and to breed up a pure, unadulterated American citizenship. I recognize that there is a dangerous lack of distinction between people of a certain nationality and the breed of the dog."[17] Not surprisingly, white supremacist organizations such as the Ku Klux Klan threw their full support behind such sentiments. By the early 1920s, the Klan was targeting Jews and immigrants from southeastern Europe for some of the same violence and terror that they had long directed at African Americans. In fact, anti-immigrant feelings of the 1910s and 1920s have been cited as a major factor in the growth of the Klan during that same period.

The Immigration Act of 1924

In 1924 Congress responded to continued public anxiety about immigration—and the relentless work of groups like the Immigration Restriction League and various labor unions—with the most restrictive immigration law in U.S. history. This law, the Immigration Act of 1924, was also known as the Johnson-Reed Act in recognition of its leading sponsors. Much of the Act had been written by Republican Congressman Albert Johnson of Washington state, who was one of the most notorious racists in Congress, and Republican Senator David Reed of Pennsylvania.

The Act had two main components. The first was language that completely shut the door on any prospective immigrants from Japan, China, and other "undesirables" across a large swath of Asia. This provision was opposed by President Calvin Coolidge, but he still signed the bill into law (see "Coolidge Signs the Immigration Act of 1924," p. 180). The second main part of the Act was a National Origins Quota, which brought most emigration from Europe to a screeching halt. Under the terms of the act, no more than 150,000 immigrants *from around the world* would be allowed into the United States in a single year. In addition, the number of emigrants from a single European country was limited, but the formula that was used heavily favored applicants from northwestern Europe at the expense of applicants from southeastern Europe.

The Act did not place any new limitations on emigration from Latin America. As a result, emigration from Mexico and some parts of the

Caribbean increased in the 1920s. Many of these newcomers took jobs in the ranching, farming, and mining industries with companies that had previously used Asians and other immigrants for their labor.

Meanwhile, countless people in Europe and Asia who had dreamed of coming to America turned away in sadness and disappointment. Many of them had family already in the United States, and they knew that the 1924 law made it far less likely that they would ever be reunited with them. In recognition of this fact, some immigrants who had entered the United States before 1924 decided to move back to the Old Country where they had been born. Others waited hopefully for the law to be amended or discarded. But it remained in place for the next 40 years.

Notes

[1] Yans-McLaughlin, Virginia, and Marjorie Lightman. *Ellis Island and the Peopling of America.* New York: The New Press, 1997, p. 56.

[2] Daniels, Roger. *Guarding the Golden Door: American Immigration Policy and Immigrants Since 1882.* New York: Hill and Wang, 2004, pp. 10-11.

[3] Quoted in Daniels, p. 15.

[4] Quoted in Daniels, p. 15.

[5] Daniels, p. 35.

[6] Williams, William. Address to the Federation of Churches and Christian Organizations of New York City, January 27, 1903. New York: s.n., 1903.

[7] Cannato, Vincent. "Coming to America: Ellis Island and New York City," History Now Online, no. 11, March 2007, available online at www.historynow.org/03_2007/historian2.html.

[8] Strong, Josiah. *Our Country: Its Possible Future and Its Present Crisis.* New York: Baker and Taylor, 1891, p. 56.

[9] Cleveland, Grover. *Message and Papers of the Presidents.* James D. Richardson, ed. Washington, DC: Bureau of National literature and Art, 1903. vol. 9, p. 758.

[10] Quoted in Chermayeff, Ivan, Fred Wasserman, and Mary J. Shapiro. *Ellis Island: An Illustrated History of the Immigrant Experience.* New York: Macmillan, 1991, p. 102.

[11] Quoted in "Roosevelt Bars the Hyphenated." *New York Times,* October 13, 1915.

[12] Hunter, Robert. *Poverty.* New York: Macmillan, 1904, p. 315.

[13] Dillingham Commission. *Reports of the Immigration Commission,* Vol. 1. Washington, DC: Government Printing Office, 1911, p. 48.

[14] Piotrowski, N.L. Testimony at Restriction of Immigration Hearings before the Committee on Immigration and Naturalization, House of Representatives, 63rd Congress, second session. Washington, DC: Government Printing Office, 1913, p. 52.

[15] Immigration Restriction League. *The Case for the Literacy Test.* New York: Henry Holt, 1915, pp. 9, 14.

[16] Grant, Madison. *The Passing of the Great Race.* New York: Charles Scribner's Sons, 1916, p. ix.

[17] Smith, Ellison DuRant. Speech before Congress. April 9, 1924, *Congressional Record, Vol. 65, 68th Congress, 1st Session.* Washington, DC: Government Printing Office, 1924, p. 5961.

7

IMMIGRATION FROM THE 1920s TO THE PRESENT

Today's immigrants and their descendents are going to remake the United States in ways more fundamental and far-reaching than their predecessors ever imagined. And that is good news for all Americans, whether their ancestors came to these shores in the seventeenth century or the twenty-first.[1]

—Immigration historian Roger Waldinger, 2004

Since the passage of the Immigration Act of 1924, American policies and attitudes toward immigration have undergone many changes. On the one hand, the United States continues to take great pride in its historic status as a nation that was shaped and guided by hardworking immigrants and their subsequent generations of offspring. This pride shone through in the 1980s, when millions of American citizens donated money for the restoration of both Ellis Island and the Statue of Liberty, which had suffered from years of neglect. But the American people have also voiced profound doubts about the economic and cultural impact of modern-day immigrants on the nation. Most of these concerns center on the problem of illegal immigration, which has become one of the most controversial political issues of the early twenty-first century.

The Restoration of Ellis Island

New York's famous Ellis Island immigration station closed in November 1954. Given the fact that millions of Americans could trace their lineage to immigrants who passed through its gates, the closure of Ellis Island attracted remarkably little public notice. This inattention continued for the next thirty years. The island was largely forgotten by both the government and the public, and its facilities were allowed to deteriorate. Vines and weeds spread

After Ellis Island was closed, the abandoned facility was allowed to deteriorate for decades.

across the grounds and buildings, and the interior of some of the abandoned structures became scarred by rainwater stains and covered with thick carpets of dust and debris.

In the late 1970s, though, some Americans finally woke up to the fact that the nation was standing idly by as one of the most significant places in its history crumbled into the ground. They also recognized that the nearby Statue of Liberty was showing signs of neglect. In response, private citizens led by automobile industry executive Lee Iacocca founded a nonprofit organization called the Statue of Liberty-Ellis Island Foundation. This organization launched a tremendously successful fundraising drive to pay for restoration of the two landmarks. Over twenty million private citizens ultimately contributed to the fundraising effort. Armed with these contributions, the foundation worked with the National Park Service, the federal agency responsible for the sites, to undertake a complete restoration of both facilities.

As the restoration effort got underway, it sparked renewed appreciation for both the so-called Mother of Exiles (the statue) and the Island of Tears (Ellis Island). "Alone, neither the Mother of Exiles nor the Island of Tears fairly represents the American story," stated a writer for *Time*. "But together, they tell something like the whole truth.… Each occupies a critical, distinct niche in the national mythology. Yet both are being repaired in the same, characteristic national fashion: a combination of technical ingenuity, can-do spirit … and ferocious patriotic pride. Two very different, very important islands—two American islands—are being redeemed."[2] And as the restoration efforts continued, they were credited with sparking a surge of public interest in America's entire history of immigration.

On July 4, 1986, the repaired and renovated Statue of Liberty was unveiled in a three-day celebration that included a massive fireworks display, fleets of historic sailing ships in New York Harbor, and speeches by the presidents of both the United States and France (which had given the statue to the United States back in the nineteenth century). Four years later, Ellis Island opened its doors to the public. Visitors flocked to the main hall, which had been painstakingly restored. Other attractions included a museum, theaters, libraries, and an oral history recording studio. Later in the 1990s, the Foundation restored two more buildings—bringing the total number of restored buildings to five—and further expanded their museum offerings. Today, the National Park Service jointly administers both of these historic landmarks as the Statue of Liberty/Ellis Island National Monument.

The McCarran-Walter Act

This restoration took place at a time when U.S. immigration law was in tremendous flux. In the first twenty-eight years after the Immigration Act of 1924 was passed, the United States did not pass any major new immigration legislation. The restrictions imposed by the 1924 Act remained in place, and immigration to America remained very low compared to previous eras in history. During World War II, some Americans called for changes that would permit Jews and other groups targeted for extermination by Nazi Germany to seek

"We have outgrown mass immigration," insisted one advocate of immigration restriction. *"It was an important phase of our national development, and played an important part in shaping who we are as a nation. But, like other phases we've passed through as a people—pioneers settling the frontier, for instance—it's something we need to put behind us."*

refuge in the United States. But an emergency increase in U.S. immigration quotas for Jews was never approved, despite growing knowledge of the Holocaust in Europe. This unwillingness to take action produced tragedies such as the ill-fated voyage of the *St. Louis* (see "Tragedy of the *St. Louis*, p. 100) and other displays of stunning indifference in Washington, DC to the suffering of Jews. In 1939, for example, Congressman Robert Wagner introduced legislation that would have admitted an additional 20,000 Jewish children into the United States over a two-year period. But other legislators changed the proposal so that the endangered children could only be admitted if the number of other Jewish immigrants was *reduced* by 20,000. These maneuvers killed any chance that Wagner's bill had of becoming law.

After the war, the United States did pass the Displaced Persons Act of 1948, which admitted 400,000 refugees from war-torn Europe. Other legislation was also passed giving additional immigration possibilities to political victims of persecution in Communist countries like the Soviet Union. But opposition to loosening most immigration restrictions remained strong among both the public and members of Congress. Meanwhile, continued reports of prejudice against immigrant families already living in America angered people like Fiorello La Guardia, the long-time mayor of New York (1934-1945) whose parents had emigrated from Italy two years before he was born. "It annoys me greatly whenever I hear thoughtless people, often raised the easy way, who have never known any of the hardships these immigrant families endured every day, hurl insults at American citizens who have in many cases contributed much more to the welfare of this nation than those who look down upon them or turn their noses up at them," he wrote. "Look around you in any part of this country: the immigrants have contributed more than their share to building its power and its wealth."[3]

In 1952 the McCarran-Walter Act was passed. This legislation adjusted the quota system for immigrants by placing greater emphasis on the ethnic makeup of America's population in the 1950s. For example, the Act stated that if 20 percent of the American people were from a particular country of origin, then 20 percent of the legal immigrants could come from that nation. The

Scaffolding surrounds the top of the Statue of Liberty in 1984. More than 20 million Americans contributed to this privately-funded restoration effort in the 1980s.

Tragedy of the *St. Louis*

During the mid-to-late 1930s many Jews living in Nazi Germany fled the country. They wanted to build new lives where they would not have to live under the shadow of German leader Adolf Hitler and his deranged anti-Semitic beliefs. But as Nazi persecution of Jewish people in Germany escalated in the late 1930s, Jewish families found it increasingly difficult to escape. Many nations had imposed strict new immigration quotas in response to the economic turmoil of the Great Depression. In addition, Nazi laws robbed many Jews of the financial resources they needed to arrange passage abroad.

By mid-1939 Nazi persecution of Jews in Germany had reached nightmarish levels, and frightened Jewish families frantically scraped together whatever money they could to buy passage on departing ships. One such ship was the *St. Louis,* a passenger liner that left Hamburg, Germany, on May 13, 1939, with more than 930 people on board—virtually all of them Jews. The passengers had applied for visas to enter the United States, and they planned to stay in Cuba until those visas were approved. But as they sailed to Cuba—which had agreed to take them in—political unrest and anti-Semitism led the Cuban government to cancel their approval for landing. One anti-Semitic rally in the Cuban capital of Havana attracted 40,000 people who cheered loudly when a government spokesman urged the crowd to "fight the Jews until the last one is driven out."

practical effect of this law was to open the gateway wider for emigrants from northeastern Europe—where most of America's early immigrants came from—and bring down the number of emigrants from most other parts of the world.

During the 1950s and early 1960s, the immigration guidelines laid out by the McCarran-Walter Act became riddled with loopholes. Congress passed several laws that benefited immigrants with special skills (such as scientists and engineers) and exempted those with relatives already in the United States from the national origin quota system. In addition, many members of Congress successfully petitioned for individual exceptions to the quota system. This method of eluding the restrictions of McCarran-Walter became common-

The *St. Louis* arrived in Havana on May 28, but all but twenty-eight of its passengers were forced to stay on board. On June 2, Cuban President Federico Laredo Bru ordered the passenger liner to leave Cuban waters. The *St. Louis* set its sights on the Florida coastline and appealed to the United States for permission to land. But even though the frightened and desperate passengers could see the lights of Miami, the administration of President Franklin D. Roosevelt never answered the passengers' request to grant them refuge.

When the United States shut its doors to them, the 900 Jews on board the *St. Louis* had no choice but to return to Europe. Jewish organizations managed to convince Great Britain, Belgium, France, and the Netherlands to accept the refugees on board. But their relief proved short-lived. In September 1939 Nazi Germany invaded Poland, triggering the beginning of World War II. Over the next few years, German forces invaded much of Europe, including Belgium, France, and the Netherlands, and set about exterminating millions of Jews living in these countries in Nazi death camps. Except for 288 passengers who found refuge in Great Britain, nearly all of the passengers from the *St. Louis* who had been refused entry into the United States were thus ensnared in the Nazis' murderous Holocaust campaign. Virtually none of them survived to see the defeat of Hitler and Nazi Germany in 1945.

Source: Ogilvie, Sara A., and Scott Miller. *Refuge Denied: The St. Louis Passengers and the Holocaust.* Madison: University of Wisconsin Press, 2006.

place; between 1952 and 1965, two-thirds of the immigrants who were admitted into the United States gained entrance through these quota exceptions.

A Major Shift in Immigration Policy

By the early 1960s, many observers believed that another overhaul of U.S. immigration policies was needed. This time, though, the primary architects were lawmakers who had been profoundly influenced by the American civil rights movement. They believed that the United States needed to do a better job of providing immigration opportunities for applicants from non-European countries. They also argued that by opening its doors more equally to all applicants, the United States would show that it was genuinely dedicated to its stated principles of equality and opportunity for all.

The Immigration and Naturalization Act of 1965 (also known as the Hart-Celler Act) ushered in a whole new era in American immigration history. It tossed aside the old quota system, replacing it with a seven-category preference system that capped annual immigration at 290,000—with no more than 20,000 immigrant visas given to any single country. The legislation also included provisions that gave special consideration to victims of political, religious, or ethnic persecution, as well as applicants with desired professional skills. In addition, the 290,000-person limit did not include immediate family members—husbands, wives, children, and parents—of people who were already U.S. citizens.

When the Immigration and Naturalization Act actually came into force in 1968, its impact immediately became clear. Emigration from Asia and Latin America increased significantly, while the number of European immigrants dropped. This shift in immigration patterns remained in place for the rest of the twentieth century and into the early twenty-first century.

The next major change in American immigration law was the Refugee Act of 1980, which expanded the number of people eligible for visas as refugees from military and political conflicts in their homelands. Six years later, Congress passed and President Ronald Reagan signed the Immigration Reform and Control Act (IRCA). This law had been crafted to respond to the rising numbers of illegal immigrants in the United States. These illegal immigrants included people entering the country by avoiding official inspection, those passing through inspection with fake documents, and those entering legally, only to later violate the terms of their visas. The most frequent type of violation committed by this latter class of immigrants was remaining in the United States past the expiration date of their temporary student or work visas (both permanent and temporary visas are issued by U.S. authorities).

RCA included many far-reaching provisions. It granted amnesty—a pardon for breaking U.S. immigration law—and legalized the presence of roughly 2.7 million unauthorized immigrants across the country. But it also imposed stiff new penalties on people who harbored or hired illegal immigrants. Finally, IRCA approved expanded patrols of the Mexican border, where most illegal immigration was taking place. The border control measures contained in IRCA, though, were not fully implemented until the mid-1990s.

In 1986 President Ronald Reagan signed the Immigration Reform and Control Act, which made major changes to U.S. immigration policies.

The Problem of Illegal Immigration

In the 1990s the issue of illegal immigration claimed an ever-larger share of the nation's headlines. By some estimates, around 300,000 aliens entered the United States illegally every year during that decade. Most of these violators of immigration law were Mexicans who believed—or at least hoped—that they could build better lives for themselves in the United States than they could in their native country. They thus undertook long and dangerous journeys on foot across desolate desert, doing their best to evade both U.S. agents and thieves and drug dealers that prowled some sections of the border country.

Some Americans believe that the steady rise in illegal immigration from Mexico stemmed in large part from IRCA's amnesty measures. They charge that the amnesty provision encouraged millions of other Mexicans to cross the border into the United States because it led them to believe that if they could just establish themselves in America, amnesty might someday be extended to them as well. Another major reason for the escalation in unlawful border crossings into the United States was the availability of superior educational, health, and other public services than those offered back in Mexico. Finally, even though most illegal immigrants were limited to work as agricultural field hands, construction workers, maids, custodians, and line workers in factories, the modest wages they earned were still far greater than what they could earn back in Mexico.

The first major backlash against these trends came in California. In 1994 the state's voters approved Proposition 187, a measure that denied illegal immigrants access to any of the state's education, welfare, and non-emergency health services. The measure won broad support by California residents who believed that too much of their tax money was going to providing services to illegals. The law was overturned by a federal court as unconstitutional before it ever took effect, but the fact that it won support from 59 percent of California voters showed politicians all across the nation that immigration was an issue they could not ignore.

Less than two years after the Proposition 187 vote, Congress passed three new federal laws. These laws were designed to put additional pressure on illegal aliens already in America, but they were also meant to discourage people still in Mexico from sneaking across the border. The Illegal Immigration Reform and Immigrant Responsibility Act (IIRIRA) and the Anti-Terrorism and Effective Death Penalty Act (AEDPA) gave the federal government new tools to arrest and speedily deport noncitizens (both legally and illegally living in the United States). The Personal Responsibility and Work Opportunity Reconciliation Act (PRWORA), though, received the most attention. This legislation, also known as the Welfare Reform Act, took away food stamps, Medicaid benefits, and other federally sponsored public benefits from both legal and illegal immigrants.

Even as these modest steps were taken to reduce the flow of illegal immigrants, though, the U.S. Congress passed other measures designed to attract greater numbers of legal immigrants. The 2000 American Competitiveness in the Twenty-First Century Act, for example, was specifically crafted to bring in foreign workers with specialized backgrounds in technology. The act increased the number of annual temporary work visas issued by the United States from 65,000 in fiscal year 1999 to 195,000 for fiscal year 2001 and beyond.

This illegal immigrant from Mexico was apprehended by U.S. Border Patrol agents when he tried to cross into the United States in March 2000.

Illegal Immigration in the Twenty-First Century

By the end of the twentieth century, the United States was still the destination for roughly two-thirds of the world's immigrants. Nearly 12 percent of the *official* U.S. population at the outset of the 2000s was foreign-born, with more than half of these foreign-born persons originating from Latin America and another quarter of them hailing from Asia. About 30 percent of these foreign-born people lived in California, while New York (11 percent), Texas (9 percent), and Florida (9 percent) also held large numbers of the national total. Analysts note that if illegal immigrants were factored in, the percentage of foreign-born born people in the American population would be significantly greater.

As the twenty-first century began, immigration—both legal and illegal—became an even more emotionally charged issue. The terrorist attacks of September 11, 2001, on New York City and Washington, DC cast a new light on the issue of immigration. These horrible attacks on American soil made it clear that immigration was not only an economic and social issue, but also a national security issue.

The attacks were carried out by 19 followers of the radical Islamic terrorist group known as al-Qaeda (including 15 hijackers from Saudi Arabia). Some of the hijackers had entered the United States using fraudulent documents; others had entered legally, but had remained in the country illegally after their visas expired. And some of the terrorists had roamed across the United States using perfectly legal visas. These findings outraged millions of Americans and prompted renewed calls for comprehensive reforms of U.S. immigration policy.

The administration of President George W. Bush responded to these events in several ways. One month after the terrorist attacks, Congress passed and Bush signed the USA Patriot Act. This legislation gave federal law enforcement groups broad new powers, including powers to monitor, detain, and deport foreigners who aroused their suspicions.

In 2002 the administration and Congress created the Department of Homeland Security (DHS), which merged 22 federal agencies and abolished the Immigration and Naturalization Service (INS), which had been responsible for handling all immigrant visas, refugee applications, requests for citizenship based on naturalization, and all other immigration issues. The INS was replaced by two divisions within the DHS: the U.S. Citizenship and Immigration Services (USCIS) and Customs and Border Protection (CBP).

U.S. national security concerns thus became increasingly tangled up in controversies about immigration policy in the aftermath of the 9/11 attacks. And in some cases, lawmakers and influential political commentators used public fears about terrorism to advance their fight against illegal immigration. In 2004, for example, a major battle broke out over the proposed Intelligence Reform and Terrorist Prevention Act. This act was intended to make changes to U.S. anti-terrorist intelligence operations, but some lawmakers tried to add provisions to make it easier to arrest and deport unauthorized immigrants from Mexico and elsewhere. They withdrew these proposed amendments, which had nothing to do with U.S. intelligence operations, only after they became so controversial that they threatened to sink the entire Act.

Calls for Mass Deportation and Border Walls

As the first decade of the twenty-first century draws to a close, the problem of illegal immigration remains one of the most emotional, thorny issues

Minuteman volunteers demonstrate at a gathering in Arizona in 2006.

roiling the waters of American politics. And feelings on both sides of the issue have proved so strong that little progress has been made in finding grounds for compromise (see "A Proposal to Increase Legal Immigration," p.185).

On one side are the millions of Americans who oppose any form of amnesty or "guest worker" status for illegal aliens. People holding this view frequently call for massive deportation of the estimated 12 million unauthorized immigrants living in the United States. Some of this fierce hostility to illegal immigrants almost certainly stems from racial prejudice against people of Hispanic heritage, who account for most of the immigrants living illegally in the United States. But it would be a mistake to dismiss all people holding strong views against illegal immigration as bigots. Many of them simply feel that illegal immigrants should not be "rewarded" in any way for breaking U.S law. In their view, proposals to give undocumented aliens paths to citizenship are nothing more than amnesty programs that would vault them ahead of the three million people who are already waiting for permanent residency visas (so-called "green cards") so that they can enter the United States. As Arizona

Republican Senator Jon Kyl declared in 2008, such proposals are "not fair to those [prospective immigrants] who've been playing by the rules."[4]

Similarly, critics insist that illegal immigrants simply do not have any right to take advantage of U.S. education, health, and other social services. They feel that giving unauthorized aliens access to these social services is unfair to the millions of U.S. citizens whose tax dollars are used to fund those programs—which in many cases are already suffering from budget shortfalls.

In addition, many of the people demanding mass deportations of illegal immigrants believe that unauthorized aliens (and legal aliens, in some cases) are a major cause of declining wages and job losses for American workers in some industries (see "A Criticism of 'Guest Worker' Proposals," p. 182). Some also claim that illegal immigrants are at high risk of turning to criminal activity as a way of rising out of poverty. Others see them as contributing to overpopulation and unsustainable consumption of natural resources. Finally, some Americans worry that both illegal and legal immigrants are eroding longstanding national traditions of language and culture. They view the rising visibility of the Spanish language in U.S. society, for example, as a clear sign that America is losing touch with its historical roots.

> *According to one analyst, "There would not be millions of undocumented workers in this country if there was not work for them to do and if there were no employers eager to hire them."*

All of these concerns have, to one degree or another, fed growing public support for the building of a massive wall along the U.S.-Mexico border to keep out illegal immigrants. These same concerns have prompted big increases in the number of Border Patrol agents in the American Southwest. Public anger and frustration has also led to the creation of citizens' militias like the Arizona-based Minutemen, which conduct their own patrols of high-traffic border areas and monitor businesses that are reputed to use illegal immigrants as workers.

Some critics of modern U.S. immigration policy also contend that immigration's historic importance in the development of the United States is no longer important. "America has changed dramatically, in good ways and bad ways, but in any case in ways that make us a mature society and render our past experience with immigration irrelevant," stated Mark Krikorian, executive director of the Center for Immigration Studies, which seeks to reduce both legal and illegal immigration to America. "We have outgrown mass immigration. It was an important phase of our national development, and played an important part in shaping who we are as a nation. But, like other phases we've passed through as a people—pioneers settling the frontier, for instance—it's something we need to put behind us."[5]

An Alternative Approach to Illegal Immigration

Other Americans, though, harbor very different views on the subject of illegal immigration. They emphasize that illegal immigrants are fellow human beings who are motivated by the same hopes and dreams that led past generations of immigrants to Ellis Island and other gateways into America (see "A Yearning That Is Timeless," p. 188). They express fear that calls to round up the millions of illegal immigrants currently residing in the United States are either coldhearted, wildly unrealistic, or both.

People holding this perspective say that children of illegal aliens suffer the most when social services are denied to undocumented migrants. They also believe that many anti-immigration proposals doom illegal immigrants to lifetimes of poverty in America, and that illegal immigrants take jobs that most Americans shun anyway. In addition, they argue that the nation does not currently have the law enforcement resources to round up and deport the twelve million people illegally living in the United States—and that the cost involved in strengthening law enforcement resources to the point where they *could* remove all illegal aliens would be astronomical.

Many of these same people view the construction of a 700-mile wall along the U.S.-Mexico border as evidence of bigotry. "There would not be millions of undocumented workers in this country if there was not work for them to do and if there were no employers eager to hire them," charged one such critic. "The record shows that immigrants' children and grandchildren learn English quickly and become productive citizens. The wall is an unprecedented physical expression of xenophobia [fear or hatred of foreigners]. Xenophobia is not new in American history, but every instance of it makes our culture more coarse and undermines efforts to think sensibly about immigration policies and to deal realistically with the twelve million undocumented immigrants already here."[6] Critics of the wall also express concern that the barrier will increase the number of Mexicans and other unauthorized migrants who die trying to cross the border, or drive them into the clutches of smugglers who have no regard for their welfare.

A Latino couple and their young son take part in a pro-immigration demonstration in Los Angeles in 2006.

Many Americans who oppose building a border wall agree that illegal immigration is a serious problem. But they believe that the government should pursue policies that give illegal immigrants already in the United States a path to full citizenship. They favor proposals that would allow illegal immigrants to become "guest workers" with options to pursue permanent residency status and eventual U.S. citizenship. Supporters argue that these types of plans do not amount to amnesty because illegal aliens must meet a number of conditions to qualify. For instance, applicants would have to learn English, be gainfully employed, pass criminal background checks, pay fines and back taxes, and agree to other conditions.

Finally, advocates for illegal immigrants argue that the United States should do more to help Mexico and other countries reduce poverty within their borders. They feel that if gains could be made in that area, then people of Mexico and other poor countries would be less inclined to make the perilous and unlawful journey into America. "[The flow of illegal immigrants from Latin America] is not a bunch of workers simply coming north to toil a few months," asserted journalist Charles Bowden. "This is an exodus of men, women, and children from nations that cannot feed them or clothe them or educate them."[7]

States Step into the Battle

The debate over the best way to end illegal immigration to the United States has created a stalemate in Washington, DC. Even the two main political parties are grappling with fierce internal divisions over the issue. Many conservative Republicans, for example, have adopted a hard-line approach that emphasizes border enforcement and deportation of illegal aliens. But other members of the party oppose this approach because they believe that American businesses would suffer if they lost this source of workers.

Similarly, many members of the Democratic Party oppose the more severe penalties and enforcement steps that have been demanded. Hispanics and other minorities are an important part of the Democratic political coalition. These groups favor policies that will give unauthorized migrants a path to citizenship, not force them "deeper into the shadows,"[8] in the words of Senator Edward M. Kennedy. But other Democrats are closely allied with American labor unions, which see illegal immigration as a threat to the wages and jobs of their memberships.

The deadlock in Washington has convinced some states to move forward with their own illegal immigrant legislation. Arizona, Oklahoma, and Missouri all passed significant immigration laws in 2006 or 2007 that sought to reduce the number of illegal immigrants within their borders. Individual cities have also passed measures to crack down on companies that hire undocumented workers. All told, the National Conference of State Legislatures reported that more than 1,500 immigration-related bills were introduced in state houses from January to November of 2007—and that 244 of them became law. Many of these new state laws, however, are facing legal challenges from opponents who claim that they are unconstitutional.

Whether these state laws stand or fall in the courts, immigration experts agree that effective immigration reform in the United States is virtually impossible without the leadership of the federal government. But as long as lawmakers in Washington are unable to find common ground on the issue, illegal aliens in America face an uncertain future.

Demographic Changes in the Twenty-First Century

Meanwhile, the ethnic make-up of the American population continues to evolve. Legal and illegal immigration, varying birth rates for different ethnic groups, intermarriage of races and ethnic groups, and other factors are all changing the demographics—race, ethnicity, and other characteristics—of the nation's population. Whites, for example, remain the dominant race in the United States in the twenty-first century. But Hispanics have surpassed African-Americans as the nation's largest minority group. In addition, the U.S. Census Bureau predicted that from 2008 to 2050 the Hispanic population will jump from 15 percent to 30 percent of the total population.

Forecasts of population growth among Hispanics, African Americans, Asians, and other minorities have created fears among some white people that whites will someday be a minority group in the United States. But the Census Bureau itself has repeatedly pointed out that "Hispanic" is an ethnic category, not a race—and that nearly half of Hispanics living in the United States identified themselves as white in the 2000 census. And many commentators have urged Americans to quit worrying so much about racial categories and focus instead on the ways in which all ethnic and racial groups contribute to the nation's vitality and growth.

Observers further note that during the course of America's existence, racial categories have changed radically. "For generations, 'whites' have been hearing that they are about to be engulfed by unassimilable foreign races, and for centuries those 'races' have eventually become—white!" observed one journalist. "In the early 20th century, federal immigration officials classified the Irish, Italians, and Jews as separate races. Yet today all these groups are viewed collectively, and benignly, as 'white.'"[9] There is every reason to think that in today's era, where millions of Americans of different races and ethnic origins are living together, marrying, and have children, racial lines will continue to blur.

These trends, say some analysts, make the United States a more welcoming place to legal immigrants than ever before. They admit that racial tensions and fears are still a problem in many parts of the country. But they also assert that most Americans no longer see ethnic or racial pride as an obstacle to American patriotism or citizenship. And there is an increased recognition that the foundations of modern American culture include materials drawn from all over the world. "America is really many Americas," observed President Ronald Reagan in 1986. "We call ourselves a nation of immigrants, and that's truly what we are....All of the immigrants who came to us brought their own music, literature, customs, and ideas. And the marvelous thing, a thing of which we're proud, is they did not have to relinquish these things in order to fit in. In fact, what they brought to America became American. And this diversity has more than enriched us; it has literally shaped us."[10]

Notes

[1] Waldinger, Roger. "The Twenty-First Century: An Entirely New Story." In Jacoby, Tamar. *Reinventing the Melting Pot: The New Immigrants and What It Means to Be an American.* New York: Basic Books, 2004, pp. 84-85.

[2] Andersen, Kurt. "A Pair of American Islands: Revitalizing a Flame and Restoring Dark Memories." *Time,* July 7, 1986, p. 22.

[3] La Guardia, Fiorello H. *The Making of an Insurgent: An Autobiography, 1882-1919.* Philadephia: J.B. Lippincott, 1948, p. 68.

[4] Quoted in Luddens, Jennifer. "Q&A: Inside the Immigration Debate." NPR-National Public Radio [online], July 30, 2008, www.npr.org.

[5] Krikorian, Mark, "The New Case Against Immigration: Interview with Jamie Glazov." *Center for Immigration Studies* [online], July 2008, available online at www.cis.org/node/689.

[6] Editors of *The Christian Century.* "Wall of Shame." February 12, 2008, p. 7.

[7] Bowden, Charles. "Exodus." *Orion Magazine,* July-August 2008, p. 27.

[8] Ibid, p. 7.

[9] Jacoby, Jeff. "The Myth of the White Minority." *Boston Globe,* August 20, 2008.

[10] Quoted in Riley, Jason L. *Let Them In: The Case for Open Borders.* New York: Gotham, 2008, p. ix.

BIOGRAPHIES

Jane Addams (1860-1935)
*Social Worker and Activist for Immigrants
Living in Urban America*

Jane Addams was born on September 6, 1860, in Cedarville, Illinois. She was the youngest child of John Huy Addams, a prominent local businessman and politician. She became very close to her father, a Quaker with a strong sense of civic responsibility, after her mother's death when she was a young child.

Addams attended college at Rockford Female Seminary, which was located just outside of Chicago, Illinois. During this period she repeatedly told classmates that she wanted to do something important with her life. She also spoke frequently about working as a doctor in a poor community. In the early 1880s, however, the life path she had charted for herself was rocked by her father's death and a mysterious illness that disabled her for long periods of time.

Founding Hull House

Addams's health returned in the late 1880s, and in 1889 she finally made her long-delayed plunge into social work. By this time, America was grappling with huge overcrowding problems in New York, Chicago, Boston, and other major cities. Within these cities, families were crowded together in tenement ghettoes that swirled with crime, disease, pollution, and desperation. Many of these grim communities were composed primarily of immigrants who had come to America in search of a better life. And although they had found jobs in U.S. factories, stockyards, mines, oil fields, and mills, the wages they received were not sufficient to carry them—or their families—out of the slums and into cleaner and less crowded neighborhoods or towns.

Addams decided to address the plight of immigrant families in Chicago by establishing a "settlement house" that would help immigrant families adjust to life in America. She and co-founder Ellen Gates Starr patterned the facility, named Hull House, after similar settlement houses that had been founded in London during the 1880s to help the poor and hungry. Located

117

on Chicago's crowded west side, Hull House offered an array of social services to Italian, Irish, German, Greek, Russian, Polish, and other immigrant families in the area. Services included kindergarten and day care facilities for the children of working mothers; legal assistance; an employment bureau; libraries and an art gallery; recreational activities for young single women; meeting places for trade unions; and classes in English, citizenship, music, art, and theater. Virtually none of these programs were available through local, state, or federal agencies, so immigrant families flocked to Hull House in huge numbers.

Addams gathered a dedicated group of educated reformers and social activists to the Hull House organization, but she was the unquestioned leader of the facility. She wrote numerous books and articles on the programs and philosophy of Hull House, and she delivered speeches all around the country on the importance of settlement houses. The amazing success of Hull House sparked the creation of similar settlement houses in many other American cities as well. By 1910, more than 400 settlement houses had been established in cities across the country.

These settlement houses provided guidance to immigrants on a tremendous array of issues, from instruction in basic American civics to keeping their homes clean and safe even in the midst of urban pollution and squalor. Addams and other settlement house leaders also lobbied city, state, and federal governments to improve workplace safety, increase trash collection and expand sewage systems, eliminate child labor, and increase welfare benefits for widows, the elderly, and impoverished citizens. In many cases, the lobbying efforts of the so-called "Hull House reformers" resulted in the creation of important new legislation that improved the lives of immigrant workers and their families. The 1912 creation of the Federal Children's Bureau, for example, came about as a direct result of the tireless campaigning of Addams and her many reform-minded supporters. Other triumphs included the creation of the first juvenile court in the nation and the founding of the Immigrants' Protective League.

A Crusader for Many Causes

By 1910 Addams was one of the most famous women in America. That same year she published *Twenty Years at Hull-House,* an autobiographical work that chronicled the challenges and victories she had experienced during her years of reform work.

As time passed, though, Addams also moved beyond her work at Hull House in her ongoing efforts to improve the lives of immigrants and the urban poor. She became a leading figure in the Consumers League, which was dedicated to establishing a national minimum wage for workers and limiting the work hours of women and children. She also served as chair of the Labor Committee of the General Federation of Women's Clubs, as vice-president of the Campfire Girls, and in leadership positions with the National Child Labor Committee and the National Playground Association. In addition, she played an important role in the founding of both the National Association for the Advancement of Colored People (NAACP) in 1909 and the American Civil Liberties Union (ACLU) in 1920.

Addams also emerged as a vocal critic of American involvement in World War I. A dedicated pacifist, she founded the Women's Peace Party in 1917. Two years later the organization became the Women's International League for Peace and Freedom (WILPF) and Addams served as its first president. In 1931 Addams was a co-winner of the Nobel Peace Prize for her peace work.

Nonetheless, Addams's pacifist beliefs and progressive ideals proved less popular in the 1920s than they had been in earlier years. Many Americans in the 1920s placed greater weight on middle-class economic prosperity than they did on issues of social justice, and they grew tired of Addams's reform message. Some Americans also viewed her as a traitor for her opposition to World War I, and critics charged that she held "communist" views on social issues. By the mid-1920s the name of Jane Addams was as likely to be met with angry condemnation as it was to be met with praise. As one historian noted, "It was a stunning fall from grace for the woman so long seen as the incarnation of saintly goodness."[1]

The attacks troubled and saddened Addams, but did not stop her from pursuing her social reform goals. She continued to oversee affairs at Hull House—which remained hugely successful—and fight for new laws to protect America's most vulnerable citizens. Health problems slowed her in the early 1930s, though, and she died in Chicago on May 21, 1935. Thousands of appreciative people attended her funeral service at Hull House before she was taken to her hometown of Cedarville for burial.

Sources:

Addams, Jane. *Twenty Years at Hull-House*. 1910. Reprint. Boston: Bedford/St. Martin's, 1990.

Brown, Victoria Bissell. "Jane Addams." In *Women Building Chicago 1790-1990: A Biographical Dictionary*. Bloomington: Indiana University Press, 2001.

Davis, Allen F. *American Heroine: The Life and Legend of Jane Addams.* Cambridge, MA: Oxford University Press, 1973.

Notes

[1] McGerr, Michael. *A Fierce Discontent: The Rise and Fall of the Progressive Movement in America.* New York: Oxford University Press, 2003, p. 308.

Prescott F. Hall (1868-1921)
Co-Founder and General Secretary of the Immigration Restriction League

Prescott Farnsworth Hall was born on September 27, 1868, in Boston, Massachusetts. Raised in an environment of comfort and privilege, he attended Harvard University in Cambridge, Massachusetts. Hall earned a bachelor's degree from Harvard in 1889 and a law degree from the school's law program three years later.

Hall joined a law firm in Boston in 1892 and worked as a lawyer for the rest of his life. His interests, however, went far beyond the courtroom. Hall, for example, became fascinated by the study of psychic and paranormal phenomena, including telepathy (mind-reading), hauntings, and other human contact with the spirit world. He was a long-time member of the U.S. chapter of the Society for Psychical Research, an organization devoted to the scientific study of such events.

A Determined Foe of Immigration

Hall was even more passionate, however, about the subject of immigration. Only two years after graduating from Harvard Law School, he joined two other Harvard graduates—Charles Warren and Robert DeCourcy Ward—in founding an organization called the Immigration Restriction League. All three of these young men believed that the United States was in danger of being overwhelmed by immigrants who did not fit into the nation's political, cultural, and social environment. Hall, Warren, and Ward were convinced that unrestricted immigration was the root cause of many of America's most notorious problems of the late nineteenth century. These problems included crime and corruption, poverty, labor unrest, and tensions between ethnic groups.

Hall's attitude was a common one among Boston's wealthy elite. During the 1860s and 1870s, they had expressed growing alarm about the increased political and economic influence of Irish immigrants in the city and surrounding region. And when the origin of most immigrants shifted from northwestern Europe to southeastern Europe in the late nineteenth century, these native-born Americans expressed even greater anxiety. The Immigration Restriction League was created in direct response to these feelings.

Hall served as general secretary of the League from 1896 until his death in 1921. During these decades he guided the organization's growth into many other large American cities, including New York, Chicago, and San Francisco. He also attracted a wide range of scholars and scientists to his cause. Many of these members were enthusiastic supporters of "eugenics," a deeply flawed scientific theory that claimed some races were genetically superior to others. Followers of eugenics believed that the flood of "inferior" emigrants from southeastern Europe and Asia from the 1870s through the early 1920s threatened the purity and progress of America's "superior" ethnic groups. Not surprisingly, the ethnic groups that the eugenics movement identified as superior—British, German, and Scandinavian peoples—were the same ones that Hall and other believers came from.

During his years at the helm of the Immigration Restriction League, Hall became one of the most powerful anti-immigration voices in the country. He effectively guided the anti-immigration efforts of the league's many local chapters, which were collectively known as the Association of Immigration Restriction Leagues. He also lectured and wrote articles explaining his conviction that the "new immigrants" were unfit for American citizenship. In 1897, for example, Hall wrote that American society had reached an important crossroads in its history: "Do we want this country to be peopled by British, German, and Scandinavian stock, historically free, energetic, progressive, or by Slav, Latin, and Asiatic races [a reference in this case to Jews], historically down-trodden, atavistic and stagnant?"[1]

Hall also devoted a lot of time to lobbying members of Congress to support the League's anti-immigration agenda. His biggest ally in Congress was Republican Senator Henry Cabot Lodge of Massachusetts. Working together, they repeatedly guided legislation through Congress that would have forced immigrants to pass literacy tests before they could enter the United States. They knew that this hurdle would keep out millions of immigrants who had not been able to obtain good educations in their native countries.

Hall rejected charges that a literacy test would be cruel and unfair. "The ability to read and write his own language does not seem an unreasonable requirement to make in the case of a man who seeks to enter a democracy like ours," he declared. "The [Statue of Liberty] carries in one hand a torch and in the other a book; and this properly interpreted means not merely that immigrants shall be educated to a higher degree after they get here, but that they should be able to read the fundamental law of the land by the light of liberty's torch in order to entitle them to enjoy the advantages which liberty has produced."[2] Despite Hall's best efforts, though, the literacy test remained just out of reach. Presidential vetoes and political maneuvering from immigration supporters kept these bills from becoming law.

Passing the Literacy Test

In 1911 the Immigration Restriction League's efforts to pass a literacy test into law received a major boost. That year a joint House of Representatives-Senate committee called the Dillingham Commission issued a 41-volume report that blamed emigrants from southern and eastern Europe for many of the nation's social and economic problems. The Commission also formally endorsed the League's call for a literacy test for aliens wishing to enter America.

Armed with this ammunition, Hall and the Immigration Restriction League renewed their demands for a literacy test. In many cases, they tried to broaden public support for the literacy test by preying on people's prejudices and fears. In 1915, for example, Hall resorted to naked bigotry in a letter to the *New York Times*. "The immigration of the last century was of races that had made good in the world's history," he stated. "Much of the immigration now coming and which will come is from races which have had all the time the others have had and have not made good. They may do so in time, but why run the risk until they have?"[3]

In 1917 a literacy test finally became law when Congress overrode President Woodrow Wilson's veto. Hall expressed great satisfaction with this victory, but he continued to press for additional immigration restrictions until his death in 1921. After his passing, the Immigration Restriction League gradually declined in influence and importance, and it eventually disbanded.

Sources:
Hall, Prescott F. *Immigration and the Educational Test*. New York: North American Review Publishing Co., 1897.

Solomon, Barbara Miller. *Ancestors and Immigrants*. Cambridge, MA: Harvard University Press, 1956.

Notes

[1] Hall, Prescott F. *Immigration and the Educational Test*. New York: North American Review Publishing Co., 1897, p. 5.

[2] Hall, *Immigration and the Educational Test*, p. 11.

[3] Hall, Prescott F. "Alien Restriction: Law Favored by More Interests Than Those of Labor." *New York Times*, Jan. 20, 1915, p. 10.

George Frisbie Hoar (1826-1904)
Republican Senator and Advocate for Immigrants

George Frisbie Hoar was born on August 29, 1826, in Concord, Massachusetts. His parents were Sarah (Sherman) and Samuel Hoar, and he was the grandson of Roger Sherman, who had helped draft both the Declaration of Independence and the U.S. Constitution. He attended Concord Academy before enrolling at Harvard College. After earning his undergraduate degree in 1846, he enrolled in Harvard Law School. He graduated with a law degree in 1849 and promptly began practicing law in Worcester, Massachusetts.

In the early 1850s Hoar briefly involved himself with the Free Soil Party in Massachusetts, but he quickly moved on to the Republican Party. He became an important state party organizer in the 1860s and 1870s, and he was elected to serve in both the state House of Representatives (in 1852) and Senate (in 1857).

In 1869 Hoar was elected to the first of four consecutive terms in the U.S. House of Representatives. During these eight years he became one of Congress's greatest supporters of black civil rights and women's suffrage. In 1877 the Massachusetts state legislature appointed him to an open seat in the U.S. Senate. Hoar represented Massachusetts in that capacity until his death, winning re-election four different times during that 27-year span.

A Friend to Immigrants

As a U.S. Senator, Hoar consistently fought for equal rights for all Americans. He believed that the Constitution guaranteed such equality. With this in mind, he was contemptuous of the American Protective Association (APA), an anti-immigration group built on a foundation of "nativism"—preferential treatment for native-born Americans and hostility toward the foreign-born.

In the late 1870s Hoar expressed particular disgust with anti-Chinese bigotry in the American West. When anti-immigration forces introduced the Chinese Exclusion Act in Congress in 1882, Hoar attacked the bill as un-American and deeply unfair to Chinese immigrants. "During Senate debate," noted one historian, "Hoar was virtually alone among Republicans in defending the rights of Chinese immigrants. In the West, anti-Chinese groups held rallies in which Hoar … was denounced and burned in effigy."[1] Hoar's efforts, though, were not enough to prevent the bill's passage. The Act choked off virtually all Chinese immigration to America for the next half-century, and it made it impossible for Chinese immigrants already in the United States to become citizens.

In the 1880s Hoar spent much of his time working on legislation to address corporate corruption. He was an important architect of the 1890 Sherman Antitrust Act, one of the earliest Congressional efforts to rein in the powerful corporate trusts that dominated the U.S. economy. As the 1890s unfolded, he repeatedly opposed the anti-immigration maneuvers of the Immigration Restriction League (IRL), despite the fact that the other U.S. senator from Massachusetts, Henry Cabot Lodge, was the League's closest Congressional ally. Hoar also vocally opposed Republican President William McKinley's military action in the Philippines, even though it was enormously popular with many of his fellow Republicans.

Hoar remained one of the Senate's great champions of immigrant rights into the early years of the twentieth century. This was an era in which hostility toward immigrants was on the rise in many parts of America. But Hoar never faltered in his belief that immigration was essential to America's historic development and its future vitality and health. In 1903, for example, he delivered a commencement address at the University of Iowa in which he declared that, in America,

> prosperity and adversity, hope and fear, joy and sorrow, come to all alike. As civilization and wealth grow, they come to read the same books and to think the same thoughts. They follow the same flag. They stand side by side on the same battle fields. The kindly charities of life melt the ice [between people of different backgrounds and origins].… I think we can affirm without doubt, if history teaches us anything, that the greatest and strongest nations always have been and always will be those that are constantly getting new blood from an unbroken stream of immigration.[2]

When he was not engaged in Senate business, Hoar pursued a wide range of other interests. He was an avid reader of English and classical literature and history, and he contributed his time and energy to the development of the U.S. Library of Congress. Hoar also served as a regent of the Smithsonian Institution for many years, and he served as an overseer of Harvard University from 1874 to 1880 and then again from 1896 to 1904. He was also known for his dedication to the Unitarian Church and his fondness for friends and family. Hoar died on September 30, 1904.

Sources:

Brown, Richard D., and Jack Tager. *Massachusetts: A Concise History.* Amherst: University of Massachusetts Press, 2000.

Tichenor, Daniel J. *Dividing Lines: The Politics of Immigration Control in America.* Princeton, NJ: Princeton University Press, 2002.

Welch, Richard E. Jr. *George F. Hoar and the Half-Breed Republicans.* Cambridge: Harvard University Press, 1971.

Notes

[1] Tichenor, Daniel J. *Dividing Lines: The Politics of Immigration Control in America.* Princeton, NJ: Princeton University Press, 2002, p. 106.

[2] Hoar, George Frisbie. "American Citizenship. Address delivered before the state university of Iowa, June 17, 1903. Iowa City: State University of Iowa, 1903.

Henry Cabot Lodge (1850-1924)
U.S. Senator and Anti-Immigration Legislator

Henry Cabot Lodge was born on May 12, 1850, into one of Boston's wealthiest and most powerful families. He was the only son of Anna Cabot and John Ellerton Lodge, a prosperous merchant whose ships traded all around the world. He earned a law degree from the prestigious Harvard Law School in 1874 before receiving Harvard's first-ever political science PhD in 1876.

Bright and opinionated, Lodge spent several years in the mid-1870s editing the *North American Review,* a leading scholarly magazine of the time. He also joined the faculty at Harvard, teaching U.S. history to undergraduate students until 1879. In the 1880s he wrote and published several biographies of famous Americans such as George Washington and Alexander Hamilton, as well as general works like *A Short History of the English Colonies in America* (1881).

Successful Career in Politics

Lodge made his biggest mark in the 1880s, though, in Massachusetts politics. In 1879 Lodge won elected office for the first time, claiming a seat in the state House of Representatives as a Republican. In 1882 and 1884 he failed in attempts to win a seat in the U.S. House of Representatives, but he remained a major force in the state Republican Party. In 1886 he finally won election to the U.S. House, where he quickly built a reputation as a serious-minded legislator who ably represented Republican interests. He easily won re-election in 1888 and 1890.

In 1893 the Massachusetts legislature selected Lodge to the U.S. Senate as a replacement for Senator Henry L. Dawes, who had decided to retire. Lodge held this seat for the next three decades, easily fending off challengers in election after election. During this time he rose to become one of the most powerful and formidable lawmakers in Washington.

Confident and ambitious, Lodge staked out bold positions throughout his senate career. He supported military involvement in the Spanish-American War and pushed to increase the size of the U.S. Navy—a position that contributed to a long friendship with President Theodore Roosevelt. He played an important role in the passage of laws designed to improve worker and consumer safety and reduce business corruption. Lodge also supported stiff tariffs on foreign goods, believing that such taxes helped protect American businesses from foreign competition. He resolutely opposed women's suffrage and voted against the Eighteenth Amendment, which ushered in the age of Prohibition in U.S. history.

Closing the Gates on Immigration

Few lawmakers spent as much time on the subject of immigration as Lodge, a native-born American who traced his ancestry back to England. As far back as the early 1890s, he spoke out against the waves of immigrants pouring into America from southeastern Europe, Asia, and other parts of the world. He declared that the United States did not have the resources to absorb all these newcomers. "Conditions have changed utterly from the days when the supply of vacant land was indefinite, the demand for labor almost unbounded, and the supply of people very limited," he said.[1]

Lodge also believed that the new immigrants were fundamentally inferior to early immigrants who had come to America from England and other parts of northwestern Europe. He felt that Americans of English descent were overwhelmingly responsible for the economic and cultural foundations of the United States—and that most other immigrant groups posed a threat to those foundations. Most new immigrants, he warned, came "from races most alien to the body of American people and from the lowest and most illiterate classes among those races."[2]

These views led Lodge to become the leading Congressional ally of the Immigration Restriction League, an organization dedicated to halting the flow of immigrants into the United States. Lodge worked closely with Prescott F. Hall and other League leaders to craft bills that would drastically reduce immigration quotas. They eventually decided that the best way to accomplish their goal was to pass a law that would require all prospective immigrants to pass a literacy test. Lodge argued that such a test would help protect America from the perils of unrestricted immigration. "It is a truism to say that one of the greatest dangers to our free government is ignorance," he explained. "We have the right to exclude illiterate persons from our immigration, and this test ... would in all probability shut out a large part of the undesirable portion of the present immigration."[3]

In 1895 Lodge was chief sponsor of an immigration restriction bill that would have required immigrants to show their ability to read and write in their own language. Vocally supported by the Immigration Restriction League, the bill passed Congress one year later, only to be vetoed by president Grover Cleveland. Undaunted, Lodge and the Immigration Restriction League continued to press for a literacy test for the next decade and a half.

In 1910 their cause received a major boost with the formation of a Congressional committee called the Dillingham Commission. This committee was charged with the task of studying American immigration policies and determining if any changes needed to be made. Lodge was appointed to the Dillingham Commission, and he played an important role in shaping the group's 41-volume report, which was released in 1911. The Commission announced that current immigration levels posed a threat to America's cultural and economic foundations, and it recommended that the United States impose strict limits on the number of people it accepted from southeastern Europe and Asia. It cited the literacy test as the best way of keeping "undesirable" aliens from entering the country.

The Literacy Test Becomes Law

Armed with the Dillingham report, Lodge once again led the fight to make the literacy test a part of U.S. immigration law. A bill containing a literacy test provision was passed by Congress in 1913, but it was vetoed by President William H. Taft. Three years later, Lodge and his anti-immigration allies passed another bill through Congress that would have imposed the literacy test. President Woodrow Wilson vetoed the bill, but this time Congress overrode the veto and the Federal Immigration Act of 1917 became law.

This act placed significant new hurdles in the path of prospective immigrants. It banned any mentally or physically disabled people from entering the United States. It also barred virtually all people from Japan and other parts of Asia from gaining entrance. But its most far-reaching provision was the long-sought literacy test. Under the law's provisions, every immigrant over the age of fourteen had to prove that they could read and write in their native language. Those who passed the test could enter the United States. Those who failed were turned away.

Lodge was pleased by the passage of the Federal Immigration Act, but he still felt that immigration laws were too lax. He lobbied for further restrictions, and he was a vocal supporter of the Immigration Act of 1924, which further reduced the already diminished stream of immigrants entering the United States.

Battling with President Wilson

Lodge's clash with President Wilson over the Federal Immigration Act of 1917 was one of many battles that the two men waged during Wilson's eight years in the White House (1913-21). Lodge supported Wilson's decision to enter World War I in 1917, but when the war ended a year later, the two men became bitter political enemies.

Lodge wanted the defeated nation of Germany to pay heavy penalties for starting the war, and he urged the postwar United States to remove itself from Europe's conflicts and minimize its overall involvement in international affairs. Since he had been named Senate majority leader and chairman of the Senate Foreign Relations Committee after the 1918 elections, Lodge was able to take these stances from a position of power and influence. But Wilson, who was a Democrat, fiercely opposed the Republican leader's foreign policy views. He called instead for ratification of his "Fourteen Points" peace plan, which did not heavily punish Germany. The president also promoted American membership in a proposed League of Nations, which would use diplomacy to prevent future wars.

Lodge organized a strong Republican rebellion against Wilson's plans. He also introduced amendments to Wilson's proposals that he knew the president would not accept. His maneuvering successfully torpedoed both Wilson's peace plan and his hopes for U.S. participation in the League of Nations. As a result, the United States did not sign a formal peace agreement with Germany until 1921—by which time Republican President Warren G. Harding had replaced Wilson in the White House.

In the early 1920s Lodge suffered from a general downturn in his health and vitality. He tried to fulfill his Senate duties but was absent from Washington for extended periods of time. He finally died in a hospital in Cambridge, Massachusetts, on November 9, 1924, shortly after suffering a stroke.

Sources:

Garraty, John A. *Henry Cabot Lodge: A Biography*. New York: Alfred A. Knopf, 1953.

Tichenor, Daniel J. *Dividing Lines: The Politics of Immigration Control in America*. Princeton, NJ: Princeton University Press, 2002.

Notes

[1] Quoted in Tichenor, Daniel J. *Dividing Lines: The Politics of Immigration Control in America*. Princeton, NJ: Princeton University Press, 2002, p. 80.

[2] Quoted in Jasper, James M. *Restless Nation: Starting Over in America*. Chicago: University of Chicago Press, 2002, p. 57.

[3] Quoted in Curthoys, Ann, and Marilyn Lake. *Connected Walls: History in Trans-National Perspective*. Canberra, Australia: ANU E Press, 2006, p. 218.

Terence V. Powderly (1849-1924)
Labor Union Leader and U.S. Commissioner of Immigration, 1897-1902

Terence Vincent Powderly was born in Carbondale, Pennsylvania, on January 22, 1849. The son of poor Irish immigrants, he left home at the age of 13 to work in a railroad yard. Four years later he became a railroad machinist's apprentice in Scranton, Pennsylvania. This training gave him valuable working skills, and in 1871 he joined the International Union of Machinists and Blacksmiths.

Within months of joining the union, Powderly emerged as one of the group's most enthusiastic members. He believed that workers had to present a united front against management if they hoped to negotiate fair wages and working conditions. Powderly thus became an energetic union recruiter and organizer. In 1874 he joined the Knights of Labor, a small secret union based in Philadelphia that had been founded only five years earlier.

Mayor of Scranton

In 1878 Powderly was elected mayor of Scranton as a member of the Greenback-Labor Party, a party that was calling for massive changes to America's currency system and institution of the eight-hour workday. He was re-elected three consecutive times by the working-class population of Scranton.

In the 1880s, though, Powderly became better known across the country for his union activities. In 1879 he was elected to the leadership of the Knights of Labor. As General Master Workman—the title given to the union's leader—Powderly immediately made major changes. He persuaded the union's membership to cast off its veil of secrecy and actively recruit workers across the country. In addition, he took diplomatic steps that lessened tensions between the Knights of Labor and the Roman Catholic Church—of which Powderly was a member.

In some ways Powderly was an unlikely union leader and politician. He was skinny and sad-looking, with a manner that came off as snobbish to many who met him. Over time, he also expressed resentment about the heavy demands that his union post placed on his time and energy. And according to one historian, "Powderly's diaries, private correspondence, and public statement reveal a self-centered and self-glorifying personality, convinced that extraordinary talents destined him to greatness and obsessed with his ... personal advancement."[1]

Rise of the Knights of Labor

Despite these flaws, however, Powderly presided over a period of great growth for the Knights of Labor. During the 1880s the union's membership soared. From 1885 to 1886 alone, the size of the Knights of Labor jumped from 110,000 to 700,000 members. Powderly's energy, his administrative abilities, and his talent for public speaking all contributed to this rise. "By the mid-1880s hundreds of thousands of Knights admired him," reported one scholar. "They carried his picture on their parade banners ... and wrote him letters asking for advice because they saw in him ... someone who expressed their fears and kindled their hopes."

The union's spectacular growth was also boosted by successful strikes against several U.S. railroads in the mid-1880s. These triumphs caused workers all across the country to take notice. Eager to be a part of Powderly's growing union machine, they signed up by the thousands.

As it turned out, though, the fortunes of the Knights of Labor fell just as quickly as they had risen. Powderly disliked strikes and preferred to negotiate with management on labor issues. This stance created a rift between Powderly and local union leaders who favored more confrontational action. The swift rise of the Knights also triggered many battles for local leadership that robbed the union of some of its vitality. Finally, Powderly's many efforts to enlist the support of the American middle class in the union cause never amounted to much.

Another issue that divided the union was the issue of immigration. Powderly and others opposed efforts to restrict immigration because they believed that the labor cause could be strengthened if immigrant workers were brought into the fold. As Powderly said, he did not want the Knights to oppose "any portion of humanity."[2] But many other Knights vehemently disagreed with Powderly because they were convinced that new waves of immigrants posed a threat to their jobs and wages.

As disenchantment with Powderly grew, many members left the Knights to join other unions, such as the American Federation of Labor (AFL). In

1893 Powderly was formally voted out of office. By that time, the dues-paying membership of the Knights of Labor had dwindled to about 75,000 workers.

Calls for New Immigration Restrictions

Powderly spent the next few years working as a lawyer, but in 1897 he was appointed by Republican President William McKinley to head up the U.S. Immigration Commission. After taking the post, Powderly abandoned the pro-immigration positions he had held with the Knights of Labor. Instead, he repeatedly and publicly urged Congress to pass new laws that would restrict the number of immigrants passing through Ellis Island and other American ports. By this time he had apparently become convinced that unrestricted immigration really did pose a threat to the wages and job security of American workers.

Like many other critics at the turn of the century, though, Powderly carefully distinguished between immigrants from different parts of the world. He repeatedly praised the contributions of previous generations of Irish, English, German, and Scandinavian immigrants and declared that present-day immigrants from those nations could easily assimilate once they reached America. But he darkly warned that most Italians, Jews, Slavs, and other "new immigrants" from Asia and the southern and eastern regions of Europe were not suitable for citizenship.

Powderly remained the head of the U.S. Immigration Commission until 1902, when he was fired by President Theodore Roosevelt. His dismissal came about after Roosevelt learned of widespread corruption and scandalous conditions at Ellis Island, the nation's most important immigrant processing station. Powderly was replaced by Frank L. Sargent of the Brotherhood of Locomotive Firemen. Powderly returned to his career in law, where he spent the rest of his days. He died on June 24, 1924.

Sources:
Oestreicher, Richard. "Terence V. Powderly, the Knights of Labor, and Artisanal Republicanism," in *Labor Leaders in America,* edited by Melvin Dubofsky and Warren R. Van Tine. Champaign: University of Illinois Press, 1987, p. 30-61.
Phelan, Craig. *Grand Master Workman: Terence Powderly and the Knights of Labor.* Westport, CT: Greenwood Press, 2000.

Notes

[1] Oestreicher, Richard. "Terence V. Powderly, the Knights of Labor, and Artisanal Republicanism," in *Labor Leaders in America,* edited by Melvin Dubofsky and Warren R. Van Tine. Champaign: University of Illinois Press, 1987, p. 58.

[2] Quoted in Tichenor, Daniel J. *Dividing Lines: The Politics of Immigration Control in America.* Princeton, NJ: Princeton University Press, 2002, p. 118.

Robert Watchorn (1859?-1944)
Commissioner of Immigration at Ellis Island, 1905-1909

Robert Watchorn was born in Alfreton, England, on April 5, 1859 (some sources indicate he was born in 1858). He was the second son born into a family of nine that supported itself through work in the local mines. Watchorn himself began working in the mines at age eleven, but the ambitious youth attended night school so that he could get an education. At age twenty-two he bought a steerage ticket on one of the great transatlantic immigrant steamers and emigrated from England to the United States.

Once in America, Watchorn found work as a miner in Pennsylvania. He eventually joined a local mine union, and in 1890 he played an important role in the founding and development of the United Mine Workers (UMW) labor union. Watchorn served as the first secretary of the UMW, and he even organized a night school for miners. In 1891 Pennsylvania Governor Robert Pattison appointed him Inspector of Factories and Mines. Watchorn spent much of the next several years fighting to curb the widespread use of child labor in America's mining industry.

During this period, Watchorn never developed the deep hostility to foreign workers that some of his fellow miners harbored. He remembered his own immigration experience and recognized that the newcomers to America's shores were motivated by the same thirst for a better life that had driven him to emigrate.

A Reformer at Ellis Island

Watchorn's efforts on behalf of America's miners and his crusade against child labor caught the attention of a number of national reformers. Leaders of the so-called Progressive Era—a period of American history in which activists fought to reduce corporate corruption and poverty and provide new rights to workers and women—identified Watchorn as a talented, reform-minded administrator.

This reputation led to Watchorn's 1905 appointment to succeed William Williams as Commissioner of Immigration at Ellis Island. Overseeing operations at Ellis Island was a major challenge, for the facility processed about 75 percent of all immigrants entering the United States at the turn of the century. But Watchorn tackled the job with enthusiasm, and, according to one historian, "the island took on a kinder, more honest, and more efficient character under Watchorn."[1]

Watchorn worked on many fronts during his four-year stint as commissioner. He spent a lot of time supervising the day-to-day operations at Ellis Island, but he also devoted time to other immigration issues. For example, he became very angry about the widespread mistreatment of immigrants after they left the protection of Ellis Island. Watchorn even approved undercover investigations of "immigrant trains" and steamships that specialized in carrying newcomers out to America's central and western states. His investigators found that the corporations operating these railroads and steamboats frequently charged immigrants outrageous fares and treated them poorly on these journeys. "I am shocked and outraged," Watchorn declared, "by the many pretexts resorted to by the opulent and powerful, and by petty grafters to squeeze the last dollars out of the immigrant in quest of work and wages."[2] These findings led Watchorn to file criminal charges against a number of railroad and steamboat operators in 1907, and his crusade reportedly succeeded in reducing some of the worst abuses.

Watchorn frequently defended immigrants against attacks on their character. He strenuously objected to charges that immigrants clustered together in urban neighborhoods in New York and other eastern cities because they lacked the spirit or ambition to strike out on their own. Watchorn argued that immigrants settled in the cities primarily for economic reasons. "The thing to do in the distant States in order to attract immigrants," Watchorn claimed, "is to offer them as good wages as they can get in New York…. The evil of congestion [urban overcrowding] is due to the fact that the immigrants settle where they are best off, as they think, and you will have to show them where they will be actually better off by distributing themselves."[3]

Watchorn also tried to improve working conditions for Ellis Island workers, who faced record levels of immigration in the early 1900s. As commissioner, he petitioned Congress to raise wages for Ellis Island employees and add staff members. He also instituted reforms to reduce employees' vulnerability to the health problems that some immigrants carried from Europe or from their berths in steerage.

Watchorn's efforts brought praise from pro-immigration groups and Progressive Era reformers. Secretary of Commerce and Labor Oscar Straus urged Congress to approve a second four-year term for Watchorn when his first term ended in 1909. But Watchorn's priorities were sharply questioned by the American Federation of Labor and other prominent unions, as well as various anti-immigration groups. They raised so many doubts about Watchorn's suitability for the post that newly inaugurated president William H. Taft withdrew Watchorn's name from consideration on March 4, 1909.

After leaving Ellis Island, Watchorn took a job with the Union Oil Company. In 1916 he founded an oil and gas exploration business based in Oklahoma City, Oklahoma. The success of the Watchorn Oil and Gas Company made its founder a very wealthy man. He gave away a good portion of these earnings, though, and even contributed a large sum of money to his hometown back in England for municipal improvements. Other beneficiaries of Watchorn's generosity included local universities, libraries, and churches. He died in 1944.

Sources:

Guzda, Henry P. "Ellis Island a Welcome Site? Only after Years of Reform." *Monthly Labor Review*, July 1986,

Watchorn, Robert. *The Autobiography of Robert Watchorn.* 1959. Reprint. Whitefish, MT: Kessinger, 2007.

Yans-McLaughlin, Virginia, and Marjorie Lightman. *Ellis Island and the Peopling of America.* New York: The New Press, 1997.

Notes

[1] Cunningham, John T. *Ellis Island: Immigration's Shining Center.* Mt. Pleasant, SC: Arcadia, 2003, p. 100.

[2] Quoted in Guzda, Henry P. "Ellis Island a Welcome Site? Only After Years of Reform." *Monthly Labor Review,* July 1986, p. 30.

[3] Quoted in *Facts about Immigration: Being the Report of the Proceedings of Conferences on Immigration Held in New York City, September 24 and December 12, 1906, by the Immigration Dept. of the National Civic Federation.* New York: National Civic Federation, 1907, p. 113.

William Williams (1862-1947)
Commissioner of Immigration at Ellis Island, 1902-05 and 1909-13

William Williams was born on June 2, 1862, in New London, Connecticut. His parents, Thomas Wheeler Williams and Lucretia Shaw (Perkins) Williams, raised him in comfortable surroundings, and he even attended school in Europe for a time. In 1885 he enrolled in Harvard Law School, where he became a regular contributor to the *Harvard Law Review*. In 1888 he earned his law degree.

Williams spent the 1890s working both as a corporate lawyer in New York City and in government posts in Washington, DC, and Paris, France. His talent and energy caught the eye of many officials and lawmakers, but most were nonetheless surprised when President Theodore Roosevelt chose him to take over operations at New York's Ellis Island immigration station in 1903.

An Unusual Choice

At the time Roosevelt selected Williams, the reputation of Ellis Island was in tatters. Under former commissioner Thomas Fitchie, operations at the facility—which processed about 75 percent of all immigrants entering America—had declined alarmingly. One investigation revealed that Ellis Island staffers had issued as many as 10,000 fraudulent citizenship papers in return for bribes. Corruption among staff inspectors was so widespread that undercover agents who infiltrated the island's operations feared for their lives if their identities were exposed. Agents also reported that immigrants were frequently served rotten food and subjected to other humiliating treatment.

The need for reform at Ellis Island was clear, but Williams was an unusual choice to clean things up because he harbored strong anti-immigration views. He believed that excessive levels of immigration were contributing to rising levels of crime, violence, poverty, and welfare dependence, as well as a general downturn in American morality and vigor. Like the Immigration Restriction League and other anti-immigration voices, Williams placed the blame squarely on immigrants from southern and eastern Europe, whom he thought were intellectually and morally inferior to earlier generations of British, German, and Scandinavian immigrants.

Williams did not shy away from these opinions after accepting the commissioner's job, either. In January 1903, for example, Williams delivered a speech before the Federation of Churches and Christian Organizations in which he declared his firm support for a "literacy test"—a reading and writing exam that prospective immigrants would have to pass before gaining entrance to America. "I am sure it will not be sufficiently far reaching to touch the real evils of the existing immigration," he stated, "[but] no further specific test other than the illiteracy test appears to be practicable as a means of keeping out undesirable immigrants.... Aliens have no inherent right to come here, and if the American people, as I think it does, wishes to exclude from the country generally undesirable people ... and those who will be obviously unfit for American citizenship, I fail to see why they should not do so."[1]

A Crusading Commissioner

As it turned out, however, Williams's personal views about immigration did not interfere with the way he carried out his official duties. In fact, Williams attacked the corruption and incompetence at Ellis Island with ferocity. He fired a number of inspectors and other employees for corruption and dishonesty, and he ordered the Ellis Island staff to treat all immigrants with "kindness and consideration"[2] or face dismissal. Williams also demolished the station's old hiring and promotion system, which all too often rewarded people for their political connections rather than their job performance. In its place, Williams introduced a system in which job security and salaries became much more closely tied to performance.

Williams also moved quickly to improve the feeding and care of immigrants. The government had hired private contractors to take care of many of these tasks, but the contractors treated the immigrants horribly. "I witnessed with my own eyes the fact that immigrants were often fed without knives, forks, or spoons, and I saw them extract boiled beef from their bowls of soup with their fingers," Williams later stated. "[The meat was tainted] and the floors were covered with grease, bones, and other remnants of food for days at a time."[3] Williams angrily responded to this discovery by canceling the existing Ellis Island food contract and giving it to another company, at a 15 percent savings.

By 1905 Williams's reforms had dramatically improved operations at Ellis Island. New arrivals at the station still faced long lines, probing inspectors, and dark fears of rejection. But at least they were not forced to endure vermin-infested facilities, spoiled food, and outright cruelty from staffers.

"[Williams's] goal," according to one history of Ellis Island, "was to make the system work efficiently, impartially, and fairly, according to federal law, and not necessarily to make it work compassionately.... [He] willingly accepted the fact that some would be turned away and might suffer terribly as a result."[4]

A Second Term

Williams returned to private law practice in New York City in 1905. He was succeeded as Ellis Island Commissioner by Robert Watchorn, another dedicated reformer. But Watchorn's tenure was marked by controversy over his pro-immigration views. By 1909 newly elected President William H. Taft decided not to nominate Watchorn for another four-year term. Instead he persuaded Williams to return to Ellis Island.

Williams displayed steady leadership throughout his second term. He continued many of the reforms that Watchorn had launched, and he attacked fraud and incompetence wherever he found it. In 1910 Williams even pursued criminal charges against a steamship company that had broken numerous laws in the "immigration trade." Fifteen company executives and employees eventually went to prison for trying to bribe immigration officials and smuggle diseased immigrants into America.

Williams retired again in 1913, and this time his departure from Ellis Island was permanent. From 1913 to 1918 he served as commissioner of New York City's departments of water supply, gas, and electricity. He then returned to his law practice, where he worked until his death in 1947. During these years he also became an avid mountain climber. He particularly enjoyed climbing in the Swiss Alps, and he wrote several magazine pieces about his mountaineering adventures in that region. Williams never married nor had any children. He died on February 8, 1947, in New York.

Sources:

Guzda, Henry P. "Ellis Island a Welcome Site? Only after Years of Reform." *Monthly Labor Review*, July 1986.

"William Williams." *Yale University Obituary Record, 1946-1947*, pp. 10-11.

Yans-McLaughlin, Virginia, and Marjorie Lightman. *Ellis Island and the Peopling of America*. New York: The New Press, 1997.

Notes

[1] Williams, William. Address delivered by William Williams, commissioner of immigration of New York, on January 27, 1903, before the Federation of Churches and Christian Organizations of New York City. New York: s.n., 1903, p. 14.

[2] Quoted in Cunningham, John T. *Ellis Island: Immigration's Shining Center.* Mt. Pleasant, SC: Arcadia, 2003, p. 99.

[3] Quoted in Guzda, Henry P. "Ellis Island a Welcome Site? Only after Years of Reform." *Monthly Labor Review,* July 1986, p. 30.

[4] Yans-McLaughlin, Virginia, and Marjorie Lightman. *Ellis Island and the Peopling of America.* New York: The New Press, 1997, p. 63.

PRIMARY SOURCES

A Labor Leader Warns Against the "Chinese Invasion"

During the mid-nineteenth century, no ethnic group faced greater hostility in the western United States than the Chinese. During the 1850s and 1860s, discrimination and racism against Chinese immigrants in America's western states and territories was blunted by healthy economic growth and low unemployment. In the 1870s, though, an economic downturn hit the region, and thousands of Chinese who had helped complete the nation's first transcontinental railroad in 1869 took jobs in other industries. These developments triggered a new surge of discrimination against Chinese workers.

In many parts of the West, labor union leaders tried to rally white laborers and the larger U.S. population against the perceived Chinese threat. One of the most prominent of these leaders was Dennis Kearney, an Irish immigrant who led California's Workingmen's Party. In Kearney's view, the Chinese workers, known as "coolies," were strange and inferior "slaves" that the big mining and railroad companies used to keep white workers weak and vulnerable. He thus called for the expulsion of all Chinese immigrants from the state. The following speech, titled "The Chinese Invasion," shows Kearney's perspective.

Our moneyed men have ruled us for the past thirty years. Under the flag of the slaveholder they hoped to destroy our liberty. Failing in that, they have rallied under the banner of the millionaire, the banker and the land monopolist, the railroad king and the false politician, to effect their purpose.

We have permitted them to become immensely rich against all sound republican policy, and they have turned upon us to sting us to death. They have seized upon the government by bribery and corruption. They have made speculation and public robbery a science. They have loaded the nation, the state, the county, and the city with debt. They have stolen the public lands. They have grasped all to themselves, and by their unprincipled greed brought a crisis of unparalleled distress on forty millions of people, who have natural resources to feed, clothe and shelter the whole human race.

Such misgovernment, such mismanagement, may challenge the whole world for intense stupidity, and would put to shame the darkest tyranny of the barbarous past.

We, here in California, feel it as well as you. We feel that the day and hour has come for the Workingmen of America to depose capital and put Labor in the Presidential chair, in the Senate and Congress, in the State

House, and on the Judicial Bench. We are with you in this work. Working-men must form a party of their own, take charge of the government, dispose gilded fraud, and put honest toil in power.

In our golden state all these evils have been intensified. Land monopoly has seized upon all the best soil in this fair land. A few men own from ten thousand to two hundred thousand acres each. The poor Laborer can find no resting place, save on the barren mountain, or in the trackless desert. Money monopoly has reached its grandest proportions. Here, in San Francisco, the palace of the millionaire looms up above the hovel of the starving poor with as wide a contrast as anywhere on earth.

To add to our misery and despair, a bloated aristocracy has sent to China—the greatest and oldest despotism in the world—for a cheap working slave. It rakes the slums of Asia to find the meanest slave on earth—the Chinese coolie-and imports him here to meet the free American in the Labor market, and still further widen the breach between the rich and the poor, still further to degrade white Labor.

These cheap slaves fill every place. Their dress is scant and cheap. Their food is rice from China. They hedge twenty in a room, ten by ten. They are whipped curs, abject in docility, mean, contemptible and obedient in all things. They have no wives, children or dependents.

They are imported by companies, controlled as serfs, worked like slaves, and at last go back to China with all their earnings. They are in every place, they seem to have no sex. Boys work, girls work; it is all alike to them.

The father of a family is met by them at every turn. Would he get work for himself? Ah! A stout Chinaman does it cheaper. Will he get a place for his oldest boy? He can not. His girl? Why, the Chinaman is in her place too! Every door is closed. He can only go to crime or suicide, his wife and daughter to prostitution, and his boys to hoodlumism and the penitentiary.

Do not believe those who call us savages, rioters, incendiaries, and outlaws. We seek our ends calmly, rationally, at the ballot box. So far good order has marked all our proceedings. But, we know how false, how inhuman, our adversaries are. We know that if gold, if fraud, if force can defeat us, they will all be used. And we have resolved that they shall not defeat us. We shall arm. We shall meet fraud and falsehood with defiance, and force with force, if need be.

146

We are men, and propose to live like men in this free land, without the contamination or slave labor, or die like men, if need be, in asserting the rights of our race, our country, and our families.

California must be all American or all Chinese. We are resolved that it shall be American, and are prepared to make it so. May we not rely upon your sympathy and assistance?

With great respect for the Workingman's Party of California.
Dennis Kearney, President
H.L. Knight, Secretary

Source: Kearney, Dennis, and H.L. Knight. "Appeal from California: The Chinese Invasion. Workingmen's Address." *Indianapolis Times*, February 28, 1878.

A Defense of Chinese Immigrants in America

During the course of the 1870s, Chinese immigrants living in California and other parts of the United States became greatly alarmed at soaring anti-Chinese sentiment. They felt that they were being unfairly singled out for discrimination and that their contributions to American society were not being recognized.

As public condemnation of Chinese immigrants escalated, some Chinese tried to defend themselves. In 1876, for example, an organization called the Chinese Consolidated Benevolent Association—better known as the Chinese Six Companies—wrote a letter to President Ulysses S. Grant asking for his help. The Chinese Six Companies was the most prominent of several social clubs and civic associations that Chinese immigrants established to help one another in the United States. These groups helped immigrants find work and housing, provided them with a safe place to socialize, and represented their interests in discussions with local and state officials. Some of these organizations even paid to ship the bodies of deceased members back to China for homeland burial.

The leadership of the Chinese Six Companies included the wealthiest merchants of Chinatown, a community within San Francisco that was mostly Chinese. These men took a leading role in raising issues of persecution and violence against Chinese immigrants with city, state, and national governments. But their appeals for equality and protection—such as this one to Grant—were turned aside. In 1882 the United States passed the Chinese Exclusion Act, which ended virtually all emigration from China and made it impossible for Chinese immigrants already living in the United States to obtain citizenship.

To His Excellency U.S. Grant, President of the United States of America

Sir:

In the absence of any Consular representative, we, the undersigned, in the name and in behalf of the Chinese people now in America, would most respectfully present for your consideration the following statements regarding the subject of Chinese emigration to this country:

We understand that it has always been the settled policy of your honorable Government to welcome emigration to your shores from all countries, without let or hindrance. The Chinese are not the only people who have crossed the ocean to seek a residence in this land....

American steamers, subsidized by your honorable Government, have visited the ports of China, and invited our people to come to this country to find employment and improve their condition. Our people have been coming to this country for the last twenty-five years, but up to the present time there are only 150,000 Chinese in all these United States, 60,000 of whom are in California, and 30,000 in the city of San Francisco.

Our people in this country, for the most part, have been peaceable, law-abiding, and industrious. They performed the largest part of the unskilled labor in the construction of the Central Pacific Railroad, and also of all other railroads on this coast. They have found useful and remunerative employment in all the manufacturing establishments of this coast, in agricultural pursuits, and in family service. While benefiting themselves with the honest reward of their daily toil, they have given satisfaction to their employers and have left all the results of their industry to enrich the State. They have not displaced white laborers from these positions, but have simply multiplied the industrial enterprises of the country.

The Chinese have neither attempted nor desired to interfere with the established order of things in this country, either of politics or religion. They have opened no whiskey saloons for the purpose of dealing out poison and degrading their fellowmen. They have promptly paid their duties, their taxes, their rents, and their debts.

It has often occurred, about the time of the State and general elections, that political agitators have stirred up the minds of the people in hostility to the Chinese, but formerly the hostility has usually subsided after the elections were over.

At the present time an intense excitement and bitter hostility against the Chinese in this land, and against further Chinese emigration, has been created in the minds of the people, led on by His Honor the Mayor of San Francisco and his associates in office, and approved by His Excellency the Governor, and other great men of the State. These great men gathered some 20,000 of the people of this city together on the evening of April 5, and adopted an address and resolutions against Chinese emigration. They have since appointed three men (one of whom we understand to be the author of the address and resolutions) to carry that address and those resolutions to your Excellency, and to present further objections, if possible, against the emigration of the Chinese to this country.

It is charged against us that not one virtuous Chinawoman has been brought to this country, and that here we have no wives nor children. The fact is, that already a few hundred Chinese families have been brought here. These are all chaste, pure, keepers-at-home, not known on the public street. There are also among us a few hundred, perhaps a thousand, Chinese children born in America. The reason why so few of our families are brought to this country is because it is contrary to the custom and against the inclination of virtuous Chinese women to go so far from home, and because the frequent outbursts of popular indignation against our people have not encouraged us to bring our families with us against their will....

It is charged against us that we have purchased no real estate. The general tone of public sentiment has not been such as to encourage us to invest in real estate, and yet our people have purchased and now own over $800,000 worth of real estate [almost $16 million in 2008 dollars] in San Francisco alone.

It is charged against us that we eat rice, fish, and vegetables. It is true that our diet is slightly different from the people of this honorable country; our tastes in these matters are not exactly alike, and cannot be forced. But is that a sin on our part of sufficient gravity to be brought before the President and Congress of the United States?

It is charged that the Chinese are no benefit to this country. Are the railroads built by Chinese labor no benefit to the country? Are the manufacturing establishments, largely worked by Chinese, no benefit to this country? Do not the results of the daily toil of a hundred thousand men increase the riches of this country? Is it no benefit to this country that the Chinese annually pay over $2,000,000 duties at the Custom house of San Francisco? Is not the $200,000 annual poll-tax paid by the Chinese any benefit? And are not the hundreds of thousands of dollars taxes on personal property, and the foreign miners' tax, annually paid to the revenues of this country, any benefit? ...

It is charged that all Chinese laboring men are slaves. This is not true in a single instance. Chinamen labor for bread. They pursue all kinds of industries for a livelihood. Is it so then that every man laboring for his livelihood is a slave? If these men are slaves, then all men laboring for wages are slaves.

It is charged that the Chinese commerce brings no benefit to American bankers and importers. But the fact is that an immense trade is carried on between China and the United States by American merchants, and all the carrying business of both countries, whether by steamers, sailing vessels or railroads, is done by Americans. No China ships are engaged in the carrying traffic between the two countries. Is it a sin to be charged against us that the Chinese merchants are able to conduct their mercantile business on their own capital? And is not the exchange of millions of dollars annually by the Chinese with the banks of this city any benefit to the banks?

We respectfully ask a careful consideration of all the foregoing statements. The Chinese are not the only people, nor do they bring the only evils that now afflict this country.

Source: Memorial of the Chinese Six Companies to Ulysses S. Grant, 1876. Available online at www.digitalhistory.uh.edu/asian_voices/voices_display.cfm?id=20.

A Native-Born American Lashes Out at East European Immigrants

As the nineteenth century drew to a close, anxiety about the impact of Eastern European immigration on American culture and economic prosperity intensified in many parts of the United States. Many influential Americans condemned the new immigrants and warned that they posed a dangerous threat to the nation's future. One of these critics was Francis Amasa Walker, a widely respected economist who had also been a Union general in the Civil War. In the 1880s and 1890s Walker delivered a succession of speeches and papers in which he described Eastern European immigrants as inferior creatures who threatened the racial purity of America's dominant Anglo-Saxon society.

In 1896, for example, Walker wrote a harshly worded anti-immigration article for the Atlantic Monthly, *one of the leading magazines of the era. He began by arguing that, since the early nineteenth century, three "changes in the national condition" had taken place that reduced America's capacity for absorbing new immigrants. The three changes he identified were a decline in availability of free public lands for settlement, the reduced need for workers on industrializing farms, and rising unemployment due to a national surplus of workers. But the heart of his argument for imposing major new restrictions on immigration—excerpted here—centered on his belief that Eastern Europeans were not fit for American citizenship.*

I have spoken of three changes in the national condition, all subjective, which greatly affect our capability of dealing with a large and tumultuous immigration. There is a fourth, which is objective. It concerns the character of the foreigners now resorting to our shores. Fifty, even thirty years ago, there was a rightful presumption regarding the average immigrant that he was among the most enterprising, thrifty, alert, adventurous, and courageous of the community from which he came. It required no small energy, prudence, forethought, and pains to conduct the inquiries relating to his migration, to accumulate the necessary means, and to find his way across the Atlantic. Today the presumption is completely reversed. So thoroughly has the continent of Europe been crossed by railways, so effectively has the business of emigration there been exploited, so much have the rates of railroad fares and ocean passage been reduced, that it is now among the least thrifty and prosperous members of any European community that the emigration agent finds his best recruiting-ground. The care and pains required have been reduced to a minimum; while the agent of the Red Star Line or the White Star Line is everywhere at hand, to suggest migration to those who are not getting on well at home. The intending emigrants are looked after from the moment they are locked into the cars in their native villages until they stretch themselves upon the floors of the buildings on Ellis Island, in New York. Illustrations of the ease and facility with which this Pipe Line Immigration is now carried on might be given in profusion. So broad and smooth is the channel, there is no reason why every foul and stagnant pool of population in Europe, which no breath of intellectual or industrial life has stirred for ages, should not be decanted upon our soil. Hard times here may momentarily check the flow; but it will not be permanently stopped so long as any difference of economic level exists between our population and that of the most degraded communities abroad.

But it is not alone that the presumption regarding the immigrant of today is so widely different from that which existed regarding the immigrant of thirty or fifty years ago. The immigrant of the former time came almost exclusively from western and northern Europe. We have now tapped great reservoirs of population then almost unknown to the passenger lists of our arriving vessels. Only a short time ago, the immigrants from southern Italy, Hungary, Austria, and Russia together made up hardly more than one per cent of our immigration. To-day the proportion has risen to something like forty per cent, and threatens soon to become fifty or sixty per cent, or even more. The entrance into our political, social, and industrial life of such vast masses of peasantry, degraded below our utmost conceptions, is a matter which no intelligent patriot can look upon without the gravest apprehension and alarm. These people have no history behind them which is of a nature to give encouragement. They have none of the inherited instincts and tendencies which made it comparatively easy to deal with the immigration of the olden time. They are beaten men from beaten races; representing the worst failures in the struggle for existence. Centuries are against them, as centuries were on the side of those who formerly came to us. They have none of the ideas and aptitudes which fit men to take up readily and easily the problem of self-care and self-government, such as belong to those who are descended from the tribes that met under the oak-trees of old Germany to make laws and choose chieftains.

Their habits of life, again, are of the most revolting kind. Read the description given by Mr. [Jacob] Riis of the police driving from the garbage dumps the miserable beings who try to burrow in those depths of unutterable filth and slime in order that they may eat and sleep there! Was it in cement like this that the foundations of our republic were laid? What effects must be

153

produced upon our social standards, and upon the ambitions and aspirations of our people, by a contact so foul and loathsome? The influence upon the American rate of wages of a competition like this cannot fail to be injurious and even disastrous. Already it has been seriously felt in the tobacco manufacture, in the clothing trade, and in many forms of mining industry; and unless this access of vast numbers of unskilled workmen of the lowest type, in a market already fully supplied with labor, shall be checked, it cannot fail to go on from bad to worse, in breaking down the standard which has been maintained with so much care and at so much cost. The competition of paupers is far more telling and more killing than the competition of pauper-made goods. Degraded labor in the slums of foreign cities may be prejudicial to intelligent, ambitious, self-respecting labor here; but it does not threaten half so much evil as does degraded labor in the garrets of our native cities.

Finally, the present situation is most menacing to our peace and political, safety. In all the social and industrial disorders of this country since 1877, the foreign elements have proved themselves the ready tools of demagogues in defying the law, in destroying property, and in working violence. A learned clergyman who mingled with the socialistic mob which, two years ago, threatened the State House and the governor of Massachusetts, told me that during the entire disturbance he heard no word spoken in any language which he knew—either in English, in German, or in French. There may be those who can contemplate the addition to our population of vast numbers of persons having no inherited instincts of self-government and respect for law; knowing no restraint upon their own passions but the club of the policeman or the bayonet of the soldier; forming communities, by the tens of thousands, in which only foreign tongues are spoken, and into which can steal no influence from our free institutions and from popular discussion. But I confess to being far less optimistic. I have conversed with one of the highest officers of the United States army and with one of the highest officers of the civil government regarding the state of affairs which existed during the summer of 1894; and the revelations they made of facts not generally known, going to show how the ship of state grazed along its whole side upon the rocks, were enough to appall the most sanguine American, the most hearty believer in free government. Have we the right to expose the republic to any increase of the dangers from this source which now so manifestly threaten our peace and safety?

For it is never to be forgotten that self-defense is the first law of nature and of nations. If that man who careth not for his own household is worse than an infidel, the nation which permits its institutions to be endangered by any cause which can fairly be removed is guilty not less in Christian than in natural law. Charity begins at home; and while the people of the United States have gladly offered an asylum to millions upon millions of the distressed and unfortunate of other lands and climes, they have no right to carry their hospitality one step beyond the line where American institutions, the American rate of wages, the American standard of living, are brought into serious peril. All the good the United States could do by offering indiscriminate hospitality to a few millions more of European peasants, whose places at home will, within another generation, be filled by others as miserable as themselves, would not compensate for any permanent injury done to our republic. Our highest duty to charity and to humanity is to make this great experiment, here, of free laws and educated labor, the most triumphant success that can possibly be attained. In this way we shall do far more for Europe than by allowing its city slums and its vast stagnant reservoirs of degraded peasantry to be drained off upon our soil. Within the decade between 1880 and 1890 five and a quarter millions of foreigners entered our ports! No nation in human history ever undertook to deal with such masses of alien population. That man must be a sentimentalist and an optimist beyond all bounds of reason who believes that we can take such a load upon the national stomach without a failure of assimilation, and without great danger to the health and life of the nation. For one, I believe it is time that we should take a rest, and give our social, political, and industrial system some chance to recuperate. The problems which so sternly confront us to-day are serious enough without being complicated and aggravated by the addition of some millions of Hungarians, Bohemians, Poles, south Italians, and Russian Jews.

Source: Walker, Francis A. "Restriction of Immigration," *Atlantic Monthly,* June 1896, pp. 822-29.

The "Horrors" of Steerage

In early 1907 the U.S. Senate and House of Representatives formed a special congressional committee to investigate the impact of unrestricted immigration on American society. This committee, which had been launched in response to pressure from native-born Americans who wanted to severely limit future immigration, spent the next four years studying the issue. It was chaired by William P. Dillingham, a Republican senator from Vermont, and included representatives from the Senate, the House, and several federal agencies involved in immigration and economic issues.

Conditions in steerage—the third-class accommodations in which most immigrants made the voyage from Europe to America—became an area of special focus for the Dillingham Commission. Steerage sections in nineteenth-century passenger ships were notoriously cramped, filthy, and chaotic. Reformers had long lobbied for new rules that would force the shipping lines to improve these facilities and take better overall care of their steerage passengers. Ironically, they were sometimes joined in these efforts by opponents of unrestricted immigration. These anti-immigration activists reasoned that if the packed steerage sections were improved, ships would be forced to carry reduced numbers of immigrants.

In December 1909 the Dillingham Commission issued a report detailing its findings on steerage conditions on transatlantic passenger ships. It confirmed that steerage conditions on many boats were horrible, and it called for new regulations to make these accommodations more humane and healthy for passengers. The following is an excerpt from that 1909 report (with original footnotes removed). Some historians believe, however, that the commission's recommended reforms can be traced at least in part to a desire to reduce immigration rather than concern for the welfare of passengers. They note that in 1911 the Dillingham Commission's final 41-volume report concluded that immigrants from eastern and southern Europe posed a significant threat to the economic and cultural foundations of American society. The 1911 report also endorsed so-called literacy tests and other proposals championed by anti-immigrant groups that would dramatically curb immigration.

It is the purpose of this report to show steerage conditions exactly as they were found, but, what is of more importance, it will show also that there is no reason why the disgusting and demoralizing conditions which have generally prevailed in the steerages of immigrant ships should continue. This has been amply demonstrated by experiences of the commission's agents, and the commission believes that the better type of steerage should and can be made general instead of exceptional, as is the case at the present time.

The report on steerage conditions is based on information obtained by special agents of the immigration commission traveling as steerage passengers on 12 different trans-Atlantic steamers and on observation of the steerage in 2 others, as well as on ships of every coastwise line carrying immigrants from one United States port to another. Because the investigation was carried on during the year 1908, when, owing to the industrial depression, immigration was very light, the steerage was seen practically at its best. Overcrowding with all its concomitant evils was absent. What the steerage is when travel is heavy and all the compartments filled to their entire capacity can readily be understood from what was actually found. In reading this report, then, let it be remembered that not extreme but comparatively favorable conditions are here depicted.

THE OLD AND NEW STEERAGE

Trans-Atlantic steamers may be classed in three general subdivisions on the basis of their provision for other than cabin passengers. These are: Vessels having the ordinary or old-type steerage, those having the new-type steerage, and those having both. In order to make clear the distinction between these subdivisions, a description of the two types of steerage, old and new, will be given.

The old-type steerage is the one whose horrors have been so often described. It is unfortunately still found in a majority of the vessels bringing immigrants to the United states. It is still the common steerage in which hundreds of thousands of immigrants form their first conceptions of our country and are prepared to receive their first impressions of it. The universal human needs of space, air, food, sleep, and privacy are recognized to the degree now made compulsory by law. Beyond that, the persons carried are looked upon as so much freight, with mere transportation as their only due. The sleeping quarters are large compartments, accommodating as many as 300, or more, persons each. For assignment to these, passengers are divided into three classes, namely, women without male escorts, men traveling alone, and families. Each class is housed in a separate compartment and the compartments are often in different parts of the vessel. It is generally possible to shut off all communication between them, though this is not always done.

The berths are in two tiers, with an interval of 2 feet and 6 inches of space above each. They consist of an iron framework containing a mattress, a pillow, or more often a life-preserver as a substitute, and a blanket. The mattress and the pillow, if there is one, are filled with straw or seaweed.... Generally the passenger must retire almost fully dressed to keep warm. Through the entire voyage, from seven to seventeen days, the berths receive no attention from the stewards. The berth, 6 feet long and 2 feet wide and with 2 1/2 feet of space above it, is all the space to which the steerage passenger can assert a definite right. To this 30 cubic feet of space he must, in a large measure, confine himself. No space is designated for hand baggage. As practically every traveler has some bag or bundle, this must be kept in the berth. It may not even remain on the floor beneath. There are no hooks on which to hang clothing. Everyone, almost, has some better clothes saved for disembarkation, and some wraps for warmth that are not worn all the time, and these must either be hung about the framework of the berth or stuck away somewhere in it. At least two large transportation lines furnish the steerage passengers eating utensils and require each one to retain these throughout the voyage. As no repository for them is provided, a corner of each berth must serve that purpose. Towels and other toilet necessities, which each passenger must furnish for himself, claim more space in the already crowded berths. The floors of these large compartments are generally of wood, but floors consisting of large sheets of iron were also found. Sweeping is the only form of cleaning done. Sometimes the process is repeated several times a day. This is particularly true when the litter is the leavings of food sold to the passengers by the steward for his own profit. No sick cans are furnished, and not even large receptacles for waste. The vomitings of the seasick are often permitted to remain a long time before being removed. The floors, when iron, are continually damp, and when of wood they reek with foul odor because they are not washed.

The open deck available to the steerage is very limited, and regular separable dining rooms are not included in the construction. The sleeping compartments must therefore be the constant abode of a majority of the passengers. During days of continued storm, when the unprotected open deck can not be used at all, the berths and the passageways between them are the only space where the steerage passenger can pass away the time.

When to this very limited space and much filth and stench is added inadequate means of ventilation, the result is almost unendurable. Its harmful effects on health and morals scarcely need be indicated. Two 12-inch ventilator shafts are required for every 50 persons in every room; but the conditions here are abnormal and these provisions do not suffice. The air was found to be invariably bad, even in the higher enclosed decks where hatchways afford further means of ventilation. In many instances persons, after recovering from seasickness, continue to lie in their berths in a sort of stupor, due to breathing air whose oxygen has been mostly replaced by foul gases. Those passengers who make a practice of staying much on the open deck feel the contrast between the air out of doors and that in the compartments, and consequently find it impossible to remain below long at a time. In two steamers the open deck was always filled long before daylight by those who could no longer endure the foul air between decks.

Wash rooms and lavatories, separate for men and for women, are required by law, which also states that they shall be kept in a "clean and serviceable condition throughout the voyage." The indifferent obedience to this provision is responsible for further uncomfortable and unhygienic conditions. The cheapest possible materials and construction of both washbasins and lavatories secure the smallest possible degree of convenience and make the maintenance of cleanliness extremely difficult where it is attempted at all. The number of washbasins is invariably by far too few, and the rooms in which they are placed are so small as to admit only by crowding as many persons as there are basins. The only provision for counteracting all the dirt of this kind of travel is cold salt water, with sometimes a single faucet of warm water to an entire wash room. And in some cases this faucet of warm water is at the same time the only provision for washing dishes. Soap and towels are not furnished. Floors of both wash rooms and water-closets [toilets] are damp and often filthy until the last day of the voyage, when they are cleaned in preparation for the inspection at the port of entry. The claim that it is impossible to establish and maintain order in these parts of the immigrant quarters is thus shown to be false.

Regular dining rooms are not a part of the old type of steerage. Such tables and seats as the law says "shall be provided for the use of passengers at regular meals" are never sufficient to seat all the passengers, and no effort to do this is made by systematic repeated sittings. In some instances the tables are mere shelves along the wall of a sleeping compartment.... When traffic is so light that some compartment is entirely unused, its berths are removed and stacked in one end and replaced by rough tables and benches. This is the most ample provision of dining accommodations ever made in the old type steerage, and occurs only when the space is not needed for other more profitable use.

There are two systems of serving the food. In one instance the passengers, each carrying the crude eating utensils given him to use throughout the journey, pass in single file before the three or four stewards who are serving and each receives his rations. Then he finds a place wherever he can to eat them, and later washes his dishes and finds a hiding place for them where they may be safe until the next meal. Naturally there is a rush to secure a place in line and afterwards a scramble for the single warm-water faucet, which has to serve the needs of hundreds. Between the two, tables and seats are forgotten or they are deliberately deserted for the fresh air of the open deck.

Under the new system of serving, women and children are given the preference at such tables as there are, the most essential eating utensils are placed by the stewards and then washed by them....

The food may be generally described as fair in quality and sufficient in quantity, and yet it is neither; fairly good materials are usually spoiled by being wretchedly prepared. Bread, potatoes, and meat, when not old leavings from the first and second galleys, form a fair substantial diet. Coffee is invariably bad and tea doesn't count as food with most immigrants. Vegetables, fruits, and pickles form an insignificant part of the diet and are generally of a very inferior quality. The preparation, the manner of serving the food, and disregard of the proportions of the several food elements required by the human body make the food unsatisfying, and therefore insufficient. This defect and the monotony are relieved by purchases at the canteen [ship store] by those whose capital will permit. Milk is supplied for small children.

Hospitals have long been recognized as indispensable, and so are specially provided in the construction of most passenger-carrying vessels. The equipment varies, but there are always berths and facilities for washing and a latrine closet at hand. A general aversion to using the hospitals freely is very apparent on some lines. Seasickness does not qualify for admittance. Since this is the most prevalent ailment among the passengers, and not one thing is done for either the comfort or convenience of those suffering from it and confined to their berths, and since the hospitals are included in the space allotted to the use of steerage passengers, this denial of the hospital to the seasick seems an injustice. On some lines the hospitals are freely used. A passenger ill in his berth receives only such attention as the mercy and sympathy of his fellow-travelers supplies....

Considering this old-type steerage as a whole, it is a congestion so intense, so injurious to health and morals that there is nothing on land to equal it. That people live in it only temporarily is no justification of its existence. The experience of a single crossing is enough to change bad standards of living to worse. It is abundant opportunity to weaken the body and emplant there germs of disease to develop later. It is more than a physical and moral test. It is a strain, and surely it is not the introduction to American institutions that will tend to make them respected.

The common plea that better accommodations can not be maintained because they would be beyond the appreciation of the emigrant and because they would leave too small a margin of profit carry no weight in view of the fact that the desired kind of steerage already exists on some of the lines and is not conducted as either a philanthropy or a charity.

There is nothing striking in what this new-type steerage furnishes. On general lines it follows the plans of the accommodations for second-cabin passengers. The one difference is that everything is simpler proportionately to the difference in the cost of passage. Unfortunately the new type of steerage is to be found only on those lines that carry emigrants from the north of Europe. The number of these has become but a small per cent of the total influx....

[The report then goes on to include comments from a woman investigator who made the trip from Europe to America on a passenger liner equipped with the "old-type" steerage quarters. Following are three excerpts from her chilling report:]

"If the steerage passengers act like cattle at meals, it is undoubtedly because they are treated as such. The stewards complain that they crowd like swine, but unless each passenger seizes his pail when the bell announcing the meal rings and hurries for his share, he is very likely to be left without food. No time is wasted in the serving. One morning, wishing to see if it were possible for a woman to rise and dress without the presence of men onlookers. I watched and waited my chance. There was none until the breakfast bell rang, when all rushed off to the meal. I arose, dressed quickly, and hurried to the wash room. When I went for my breakfast, it was no longer being served. The steward asked why I hadn't come sooner saying 'The bell rang at 5 minutes to 7 and now it is 20 after.' I suggested that twenty-five minutes wasn't a long time for serving 160 people, and also explained the real reason of my tardiness. He then said that under the circumstances I could still have some bread. However, he warned me not to use that excuse again. As long as no systematic order is observed in serving food in the steerage, the passengers will resort to the only effective method they know. Each will rush to get his share...."

"The manner in which the sailors, stewards, firemen, and others mingled with the women passengers was thoroughly revolting. Their language and the topics of their conversation were vile. Their comments about the women, and made in their presence, were coarse. What was far worse and of continual occurrence was their handling the women and girls. Some of the crew were always on deck, and took all manner of liberties with the women, in broad daylight as well as after dark.

"Not one young woman in the steerage escaped attack. The writer herself was no exception. A hard, unexpected blow in the offender's face in the presence of a large crowd of men, an evident acquaintance with the stewardess, doctor, and other officers, general experience, and manner were all required to ward off further attacks. Some few of the women, perhaps, did not find these attentions so disagreeable; some resisted them for a time, then weakened; some fought with all their physical strength, which naturally was powerless against a man's. Others were continually fleeing to escape. Two more refined and very determined Polish girls fought the men with pins and teeth, but even they weakened under this continued warfare and needed some moral support about the ninth day. The atmosphere was one of general lawlessness and total disrespect for women. It naturally demoralized the women themselves after a time. There was no one to whom they might appeal. Besides, most of them did not know the official language on the steamer, nor were they experienced enough to know they were entitled to protection...."

"To sum up, let me make some general statements that will give an idea of the awfulness of steerage conditions on the steamer in question. During these twelve days in the steerage I lived in a disorder and in surroundings that offended every sense. Only the fresh breeze from the sea overcame the sickening odors. The vile language of the men, the screams of the women defending themselves, the crying of children, wretched because of their surroundings, and practically every sound that reached the ear, irritated beyond endurance. There was no sight before which the eye did not prefer to close. Everything was dirty, sticky, and disagreeable to the touch. Every impression was offensive. Worse than this was the general air of immorality. For fifteen hours each day I witnessed all around me this improper, indecent, and forced mingling of men and women who were total strangers and often did not understand one word of the same language. People can not live in such surroundings and not be influenced."

Source: "Steerage Conditions," Partial Report, on Behalf of the Immigration Commission, on Steerage Conditions. U.S. Senate Document no. 206. Washington, DC: Government Printing Office, 1909.

A Long and Difficult Journey

During the great wave of immigration of the late 1800s and early 1900s, one of the greatest trials of any immigrant's move to the United States was the trip itself. For millions of people living deep inside Europe, just reaching a European port was a long and exhausting journey that could take days or weeks. Once they got to the ship that would take them across the Atlantic Ocean to America, most of them faced long days in steerage, where seasickness-inducing storms, overcrowding, and unsanitary conditions could make even the hardiest passengers question their decision. And when they finally reached America, every immigrant wondered anxiously whether they would be turned away by U.S. immigration officials.

In 1913 Scottish historian Stephen Graham decided to book passage on one of Europe's great immigrant ships so that he could study the immigration experience firsthand. The following is an excerpt from With Poor Immigrants in America, *his 1914 account of his voyage, his passage through Ellis Island, and his impressions of immigrant life in the United States. The excerpt begins with the author's arrival in London, through which many immigrants passed on their way to England's main transatlantic port in Liverpool.*

A long procession of Russian peasants was just filing out from the miserable steamship *Perm.* They were in black, white, and brown sheepskins and in astrakhan hats, some in blue blouses and peak-hats, some in brightly embroidered linen shirts; none wore collars, but some had new shiny bowlers, on which the litter and dust of the port was continually falling.... The women wore sheepskins also, many of them, and their heads were covered with shawls; they had their babies sewn up in little red quilts. Beside them there were pretty town girls and Jewesses dressed in cotton and serges and cheap hats. There were few old people and many young ones, and they carried under their arms clumsy, red-painted wooden boxes and baskets from which kettles and saucepans dangled. On their backs they had sacks, and in their hands several of them had crusts of bread picked up in their hurry as they were hustled from their berths and through the mess-room. Some of the sacks on their backs, as I afterward saw, contained nothing but crusts of white and black bread, on which, perhaps, they trusted to live during the first weeks in America!

They were all rather bewildered for the moment, and a trifle anxious about the Customs officers.

"What is this town?" they asked.

"For what are the Customs men looking?"

"Where is our agent—the man they said would be here?"

I entered into conversation with them, and over and over again answered the question, "What is this town?" I told them it was London.

"Is it a beautiful town?" they asked.

"Is it a large town?"

"Do we have to go in a train [to Liverpool]?"

"How far is it?"

"Look at my ticket; what does it say?"

They made a miscellaneous crowd on the quay-side, and I talked to them freely, answered their questions, and in turn put questions of my own. They came from all parts of Russia, even from remote parts, and were going to just as diverse places in America: to villages in Minnesota, in Michigan, in Iowa; to Brooklyn, to Boston, to Chicago. I realised the meaning of the phrase, "the magic word Chicago." I told them how many people there were in London, how much dock labourers got a week, pointed out the Tower Bridge, and calmed them about the non-appearance of their agent. I knew him, and if he didn't turn up I would lead them to him. They might be calm; he knew Russian, he would arrange all for them....

They were all going [to America] from Liverpool, some by the Allan Line, some by the White Star, and others by the Cunard. As by far the greatest number were going on the Cunard boat, I ... booked a passage on that line. There was much to arrange and write, my sack to pack, and many good-byes to utter—all in the briefest space of time.

At midnight I returned to the station and took my seat in the last train for Liverpool. Till the moment before departure I had a compartment to myself; but away down at the back of the train were coach after coach of Russians, all stretched on their sheepskins on the narrow seats and on the floor, with their children in the string cradles of the parcel-racks. They were crowded with bundles and baskets and kettles and saucepans, and yet they had disposed themselves to sleep. As I walked along the corridor I heard the chorus of heavy breathing and snoring. In one of the end carriages a woman was on her knees praying—prostrating and crossing herself. As we moved out of St. Pancras [train station in London] I felt as I did when upon the pilgrim boat going to Jerusalem, and I said to myself with a thrill, "We have mysterious passengers on board." The sleeping Russians gave an atmosphere to the English train. It was like the peculiar feeling that comes to the other people in a house when news is given downstairs that a new baby has arrived....

In a thunderstorm, with a high gale and showers of blinding hail and snow, with occasional flashing forth of amazing sunshine, to be followed by deepest gloom of threatening cloud, we collected on the quay at Liverpool-English, Russians, Jews, Germans, Swedes, Finns—all staring at one another curiously, and trying to understand languages we had never heard before. Three hundred yards out in the harbour stood the red-funneled Cunarder which was to bear us to America; and we waited impatiently for the boat which should take us alongside. We carried baskets and portmanteaus [leather suitcases] in our strained hands; most of us were wearing heavy cloaks, and some had sacks upon their backs, so we were all very ready to rush aboard the ferry-boat and dump our burdens on its damp decks. What a stampede there was—people pushing into portmanteaus, baskets pushing into people! At last we had all crossed the little gangway, and all that remained on shore were the few relatives and friends who had come to see the English off....

Then away we went over the water, and thoughts of England passed rapidly away in the interest of coming nearer to civilisation's toy, the great liner. We felt the romance of ocean travel, and also the tremulous fear which the ocean inspires. Then as we lay in the lee of the vast, steep, blood- and soot-coloured liner, each one of us thought of the *Titanic* and the third-class passengers who went down beneath her into the abyss.

The vastness of the liner made our ferry-boat look like a matchbox. A door opened in the great red wall and a little gangway came out of it like a tongue coming out of a mouth. We all picked up our bags and baggage and pushed and squirmed along this narrow footway that led into the mouth of the steamer and away down into its vast, cavernous, hungry stomach: English, Russians, Jews, Germans, Poles, Swedes, Finns, Flemings, Spaniards, Italians, Canadians, passed along and disappeared—among them all, I myself.

There were fifteen hundred of us; each man and woman, still carrying handbags and baskets, filed past a doctor and two assistants, and was cursorily examined for diseases of the eye or skin.

"Hats and gloves off!" was our first greeting on the liner. We marched slowly up to the medical trio, and each one as he passed had his eyelid seized by the doctor and turned inside out with a little instrument. It was a strange liberty to take with one's person; but doctors are getting their own way nowadays, and they were looking for *trachoma*. For the rest the passing of hands through our hair and examination of our skin for signs of scabies was not so rough, and the cleaner-looking people were not molested.

Still carrying our things we took our medical-inspection cards and had them stamped by a young man on duty for that purpose. Then we were shown our berths.

There was a spring bed for each person, a towel, a bar of soap, and a life-preserver. The berths were arranged, two, four, and six in a cabin. Married couples could have a room to themselves, but for the rest men and women were kept in different sets of cabins. British were put together, Scandinavians together, Russians and Jews together. It was so arranged that the people in the cabins understood one another's language. Notices on the walls warned that all emigrants would be vaccinated on deck, whether they had been vaccinated before or not; that all couples making love too warmly would be married compulsorily at New York if the authorities deemed it fit, or should be fined or imprisoned; that in case of fire or smoke being seen anywhere we were to report to chief steward, but not to our fellow-passengers; that smoking was not allowed except on the upper deck, and so on. The cabins were a glittering, shining white; they were small and box-like; they possessed wash-basins and water for the first day of the voyage, but not to be replenished on succeeding days. There were general lavatories where you might wash in hot or cold water, and there were bath-rooms which were locked and never used. Each cabin had a little mirror. The cabins were steam-heated, and when the passengers were dirty the air was foul. Fresh air was to be found on the fore and after decks, except in time of storm, when we were barred down. In time of storm the smell below was necessarily worse—atrocious, for most of the people were very sick.

We had, however, a great quantity of dark space to ourselves, and could prowl into the most lonesome parts of the vessel. The dark recesses were always occupied by spooning couples who looked as if they had embarked on this journey only to make love to one another. There were parts of the ship wholly given over to dancing, other parts to horse-play and feats of strength. There was an immense dining-room with ante-chambers and there, to the sound of the jangling dinner-bell echoing and wandering far or near over the ship, we assembled to meals.

The emigrants flocked into the mess-room from the four doors to twenty immense tables spread with knives and forks and toppling platters of bread. Nearly all the men came in in their hats—in black glistening ringlety sheepskin hats, in fur caps, in bowlers, in sombreros, in felt hats with high crowns, in Austrian cloth hats, in caps so green that the wearer could only be Irish. Most of the young men were curious to see what girls there were on board, and looked eagerly to the daintily clad Swedish women, blonde and auburn-haired beauties in tight-fitting, speckless jerseys. The British girls came in in their poor cotton dresses, or old silk ones, things that had once looked grand for Sunday wear but now bore miserable crippled hooks and eyes, threadbare seams, gaping fastenings—cheerful daughters of John Bull [a symbol of England] trapesing [traipsing] along in the shabbiest of floppy old boots. Then there were the dark and somewhat forward Jewesses, talking animatedly with little Jew men in queer-shaped trousers and skimpy coats; there were slatternly looking Italian women with their children, intent on being at home in whatever circumstances. There was a party of shapely and attractive Austrian girls that attracted attention from the others and a regular scramble to try to sit next to them or near them. No one ever saw a greater miscellaneity and promiscuity of peoples brought together by accident. I sat between a sheepskin-wrapped peasant wife from the depths of Russia and a neat Danish engineer, who looked no different from British or American. Opposite me were two cowboys going back to the Far West, a dandified Spanish Jew sat next to them on one hand and two Norwegians in voluminous knitted jackets on the other. At the next table was a row of boisterous Flemings, with huge caps and gaudy scarfs. There were Americans, spruce and smart and polite; there were Italians, swarthy and dirty, having their black felt hats on their heads all through the meal and resting their elbows on the table as if they'd just come into a public-house in their native land. There were gentle youths in shirts which womenfolk had embroidered in Little Russia; there were black-bearded Jewish patriarchs in their gabardines, tall and gaunt.

A strange gathering of seekers, despairers, wanderers, pioneers, criminals, scapegoats. I thought of all the reasons that had brought these various folk together to make a community, that had brought them all together to form a Little America. From Great Britain it is so often the drunkard who is sent. Some young fellow turns out to be wilder than the rest of his family; he won't settle down to the sober, righteous, and godly life that has been the destiny of the others; he is likely to disgrace respectability, so parents or friends give him his passage-money and a little capital and send him away across the sea. Henceforth his name is mentioned at home with a 'ssh, or with a tear—till the day that he makes his fortune. With the drunkard go the young forger or embezzler whose shame has been covered up and hidden, but who can get no "character" [reference] from his last employer. Then there are the unemployed, and those discontented with their jobs, the out-of-works, the men who have seen no prospect in the old land and felt no freedom. There are the wanderers, the rovers, the wastrels, so called, who have never been able to settle down; there are also the prudent and thoughtful men who have read of better conditions and go simply to take advantage of them. There are those who are there almost against their will, persuaded by the agents of the shipping companies and the various people interested to keep up the flow of people into America. There are the women who are going out to their sweethearts to be married, and the wives who are going to the husbands who have "made good"; there are the girls who have got into trouble at home and have slid away to America to hide their shame; there are girls going to be domestic servants, and girls doomed to walk the streets—all sitting down together, equals, at a table where no grace is said but the whisper of hope which rises from each heart....

[Finally, after long days at sea, Graham and the rest of his fellow passengers draw near to the American coastline.]

Sunday was Easter Day, and I was up in the dark hours of the morning and saw the dawn. Sunrise showed the clouds in the east, but in north and south and west the other clouds still lay asleep. Up on the after-deck of the great tireless steamer little groups of cloaked and muffled emigrants stood gazing over the now familiar ocean. We knew it was our last day on the ship, and that before the dawn on the morrow we should be at the American shore. How fittingly was it Easter, first day of resurrection, festive day of spring, day of promise and hope, the anniversary of happy days, of first communions! ...

"Will there be any [religious] service in the steerage to-day?"

"No, there will only be service for first- and second-class passengers."

"Is that because they need it more than we?"

There was no answer to that impolite remark. Still it was rather amusing to find that the Church's office was part of the luxury of the first and second class.

The third class played cards and danced and sang and flirted as usual. They had need of blessing.

So at night a Baptist preacher organised a prayer-meeting on his own account, and the English-speaking people sang "Onward, Christian soldiers," in a rather half-hearted way at eight o'clock, and "Jesus, lover of my soul, let me to Thy Bosom fly," at nine; and there was a prayer and a sermon.

A few hours after I had lain down to sleep Maxim Holost put his head in at my cabin and cried out:

"America! Come up and see the lights of America."

And without waiting for me to follow, he rushed away to say the same thing to others, "America! America!" …

The day of the emigrants' arrival in New York was the nearest earthly likeness to the final Day of Judgment, when we have to prove our fitness to enter Heaven. Our trial might well have been prefaced by a few edifying reminders from a priest.

It was the hardest day since leaving Europe and home. From 5 A.M., when we had breakfast, to three in the afternoon, when we landed at the Battery, we were driven in herds from one place to another, ranged into single files, passed in review before doctors, poked in the eyes by the eye-inspectors, cross-questioned by the pocket-inspectors, vice detectives, and blue-book compilers.

Nobody had slept the night before. Those who approached America for the first time stood on the open deck and stared at the lights of Long Island. Others packed their trunks. Lovers took long adieus and promised to write one another letters. There was a hum of talking in the cabins, a continual pattering of feet in the gangways, a splashing of water in the lavatories where cleanly emigrants were trying to wash their whole bodies at hand-basins. At last the bell rang for breakfast: we made that meal before dawn. When it was finished we all went up on the forward deck to see what America looked like by morning light. A little after six we were all chased to the after-deck and made to file past two detectives and an officer. The detectives eyed us; the officer counted to see that no one was hiding.

At seven o'clock our boat lifted anchor and we glided up the still waters of the harbour. The whole prow was a black mass of passengers staring at the ferry-boats, the distant factories, and sky-scrapers. Every point of vantage was seized, and some scores of emigrants were clinging to the rigging. At length we came into sight of the green-gray statue of Liberty, far away and diminutive at first, but later on, a celestial figure in a blaze of sunlight. An American waved a starry flag in greeting, and some emigrants were disposed to cheer, some shed silent tears. Many, however, did not know what the statue was. I heard one Russian telling another that it was the tombstone of Columbus.

We carried our luggage out at eight, and in a pushing crowd prepared to disembark. At 8:30 we were quick-marched out of the ship to the Customs Wharf and there ranged in six or seven long lines. All the officials were running and hustling, shouting out, "Come on!" "Hurry!" "Move along!" and clapping their hands. Our trunks were examined and chalk-marked on the run—no delving for diamonds—and then we were quick-marched further to a waiting ferry-boat. Here for the time being hustle ended. We waited three-quarters of an hour in the seatless ferry, and every one was anxiously speculating on the coming ordeal of medical and pocket examination. At a quarter to ten we steamed for Ellis Island. We were then marched to another ferry-boat, and expected to be transported somewhere else, but this second vessel was simply a floating waiting-room. We were crushed and almost suffocated upon it. A hot sun beat upon its wooden roof; the windows in the sides were fixed; we could not move an inch from the places where we were awkwardly standing, for the boxes and baskets were so thick about our feet; babies kept crying sadly, and irritated emigrants swore at the sound of them. All were thinking—"Shall I get through?" "Have I enough money?" "Shall I pass the doctor?" and for a whole hour, in the heat and noise and discomfort, we were kept thinking thus. At a quarter-past-eleven we were released in detachments. Every twenty minutes each and every passenger picked up his luggage and tried to stampede through with the party, a lucky few would bolt past the officer in charge, and the rest would flood back with heart-broken desperate looks on their faces. Every time they failed to get included in the outgoing party the emigrants seemed to feel that they had lost their chance of a job, or that America was a failure, or their coming there a great mistake. At last, at quarter-past twelve, it was my turn to rush out and find what Fate and America had in store for me.

Once more it was "Quick march!" and hurrying about with bags and baskets in our hands, we were put into lines. Then we slowly filed up to a doctor who turned our eyelids inside out with a metal instrument. Another doctor scanned faces and hands for skin diseases, and then we carried our ship-inspection cards to an official who stamped them. We passed into the vast hall of judgment, and were classified and put into lines again, this time according to our nationality. It was interesting to observe at the very threshold of the United States the mechanical obsession of the American people. This ranging and guiding and hurrying and sifting was like nothing so much as the screening of coal in a great breaker tower.

It is not good to be like a hurrying, bumping, wandering piece of coal being mechanically guided to the sacks of its type and size, but such is the lot of the immigrant at Ellis Island....

Source: Graham, Stephen. *With Poor Immigrants in America.* New York: Macmillan, 1914, pp. 3-4, 7-14, 38-44.

Forging a New Identity in America

Every immigrant's experience in America was unique. Some thrived in their adopted country, while others experienced years of disappointment and heartbreak. Millions disappeared into America's great cities of the east, while millions of others headed west to establish themselves. And although many immigrants found jobs and raised their families in ethnic communities and neighborhoods, many others left the familiarity and security of these enclaves in their search for financial and spiritual fulfillment.

Marcus Eli Ravage was one of the immigrants to America whose quest for a better life took him far away from the ethnic immigrant neighborhoods that many of his fellow travelers chose. A Jew raised in Romania, Ravage left his homeland for the United States in 1900, at just sixteen years of age. He never saw his parents again. After reaching America, he found work in a textile workshop in New York and found companionship with friends and relatives who had also emigrated from Romania. But he later left his Romanian Jewish neighborhood in New York to attend school at the University of Missouri in Columbia. He then became a journalist and part-time rabbi.

The following excerpt is from An American in the Making, *Ravage's 1917 memoir of his immigration experience. In the first part of the excerpt, Ravage explains how difficult it was for immigrants to learn American ways. In the second part, he discusses how his university experience led him to leave New York City behind and forge a new "American" identity.*

Oh, if I could show you America as we of the oppressed peoples see it! If I could bring home to you even the smallest fraction of this sacrifice and this upheaval, the dreaming and the strife, the agony and the heartache, the endless disappointments, the yearning and the despair—all of which must be ours before we can make a home for our battered spirits in this land of yours. Perhaps, if we be young, we dream of riches and adventure, and if we be grown men we may merely seek a haven for our outraged human souls and a safe retreat for our hungry wives and children. Yet, however aggrieved we may feel toward our native home, we cannot but regard our leaving it as a violent severing of the ties of our life, and look beyond toward our new home as a sort of glorified exile. So, whether we be young or old, something of ourselves we always leave behind in our hapless, cherished birthplaces. And the heaviest share of our burden inevitably falls on the loved ones that remain when we are gone. We make no illusions for ourselves. Though we may expect wealth, we have no thought of returning. It is farewell forever. We are not setting out on a trip; we are emigrating. Yes, we are emigrating, and there is our experience, our ordeal, in a nutshell. It is the one-way passport for us every time. For we have glimpsed a vision of America, and we start out resolved that, whatever the cost, we shall make her our own. In our heavy-laden hearts we are already Americans. In our own dumb way we have grasped her message to us.

Yes, we immigrants have a real claim on America. Every one of us who did not grow faint-hearted at the start of the battle and has stuck it out has earned a share in America by the ancient right of conquest. We have had to subdue this new home of ours to make it habitable, and in conquering it we have conquered ourselves. We are not what we were when you saw us landing from the Ellis Island ferry. Our own kinsfolk do not know us when they come over. We sometimes hardly know ourselves....

It seems to be assumed by the self-complacent native that we immigrants are at once and overwhelmingly captivated by America and all things American. The mere sight of this new world, he fancies, should fill our hearts with the joy of dreams realized and leave us in a state of surfeited contentment, empty of all further desire. Why, he would ask, if the doubt were ever to occur to him—why should we not be happy? Have we not left our own country because we were in one way or another discontented there? And if we have chosen America, it is quite clear that we must have been attracted by what she offered us in substitution. Besides, no man with eyes could fail to see right off the superiority of this great Republic to every other country on the face of the earth. Witness how the tide of immigration is forever flowing—and always in one direction. If the alien were dissatisfied with America, would he not be taking the first steamer back instead of inviting his friends and family to follow him?

And yet, in spite of logic and appearances, the truth remains that the immigrant is almost invariably disappointed in America. At any rate, of this much I am certain: I myself was very bitterly disappointed in America. And, unless observation has been altogether astray with me, I think I am justified in the generalization that nearly all other new-comers are at least as disappointed as I was. It was not that this land of my aspirations had failed to come up to my dream of it, although in a measure it did fall short there. Neither was my disillusionment due to the dreariness, the sordidness, and the drudgery of immigrant life, although this, too, may have entered into the equation. All these things came only later. I am writing of the first impact of America—or of that small fraction of it which was America to me—of the initial shock that came to me when I first set foot on American soil. And I say that long before I had had time to find out what my own fate would be in this new world, I experienced a revulsion of feeling of the most distressful sort.

What were the reasons for it? Well, there were a variety of them: To begin with, the alien who comes here from Europe is not the raw material that Americans suppose him to be. He is not a blank sheet to be written on as you see fit. He has not sprung out of nowhere. Quite the contrary. He brings with him a deep-rooted tradition, a system of culture and tastes and habits—a point of view which is as ancient as his national experience and which has been engendered in him by his race and his environment. And it is this thing—this entire Old World soul of his—that comes in conflict with America as soon as he has landed. Not, I beg you to observe, with America of the Americans; not, at any rate, immediately. Of that greater and remoter world in which the native resides we immigrants are for a long time hardly aware. What rare flashes of it do come within range of our blurred vision reveal a planet so alien and far removed from our experience that they strike us as merely comical or fantastic—a set of phenomena so odd that we can only smile over them but never be greatly concerned with them....

On the whole, I take it, the foreign colony in our larger cities is a little unfavorably regarded by the conventional enthusiasts for Americanization. These kindly ladies and gentlemen appear to assume that the trick of turning American is some kind of an affair of a rubber stamp and an oath of allegiance and bath-tubs. It is quite simple. You go down there, to the East Side, or Little Italy, or Little Poland, and you establish a settlement and deliver lectures and furnish them a pointed example, and behold! the fog lifts, and before your eyes stands the new-born American. The sooner this effective performance is accomplished the better, for it is quite clear that the immigrant invariably hails from an inferior world, with queer notions about manners and the use of soap and fresh air and constitutions, and if he is long left to himself and his fellows he will settle down to this pestiferous imported life of his and never become one of us at all. He will become a confirmed alien, a dangerous, disruptive element.

Into this complacent view the patent fact that Americanism is a compromise does not enter. It is quite overlooked that the adoptive American has always been and will always remain a composite American. My good friends are unwilling to see that the alien has as much to teach as to learn, that his readjustment is inevitably a matter of give and take, and that he only begins to feel at home in this new country when he has succeeded in blending his own culture and ideas and mode of life with those of the people that came here before him. Your self-complacent native takes stock of the Americanized alien and cries, delightedly, "See how America has changed him!" But I suppose he would be greatly astonished if the immigrant were to answer, with equal truth, "Look how I have changed America!" …

[Ravage saved up enough money to attend the University of Missouri for a year. Unsure of himself, he struggled to make friends with his fellow students, most of whom had been born and raised in America. At the end of his freshman year Ravage returned to New York City, where other family members lived and where he hoped to earn money for a second year of study at Missouri. Upon returning to his old neighborhood, however, Ravage realized that his year out west had changed him forever.]

So to New York I went, and lived through the last and the bitterest episode in the romance of readjustment. During that whole strenuous year [at Missouri], while I was fighting my battle for America, I had never for a moment stopped to figure the price it was costing me. I had not dreamed that my mere going to Missouri had opened up a gulf between me and the world I had come from, and that every step I was taking toward my ultimate goal was a stride away from everything that had once been mine, that had once been myself. Now, no sooner had I alighted from the train than it came upon me with a pang that that one year out there had loosened ties that I had imagined were eternal.

There was [brother] Paul faithfully at the ferry, and as I came off he rushed up to me and threw his arms around me and kissed me affectionately. Did I kiss him back? I am afraid not. He took the grip [suitcase] out of my hand and carried it to the Brooklyn Bridge. Then we boarded a car. I asked him where we were going, and he said, mysteriously, "To Harry's." A surprise was awaiting me, apparently. As we entered the little alley of a store in the Italian quarter I looked about me and saw no one. But suddenly there was a burst of laughter from a dozen voices, a door or two opened violently, and my whole family was upon me—brothers, a new sister-in-law, cousins of various degrees, some old people, a few children. They rushed me into the apartment behind the store, pelting me with endearments and with questions. The table was set as for a Purim [a Jewish holiday] feast. There was an odor of pot-roasted chicken, and my eye caught a glimpse of chopped eggplant. As the meal progressed my heart was touched by their loving thoughtfulness.

Nothing had been omitted—not even the red wine and the Turkish peas and rice. Harry and every one else kept on urging me to eat. "It's a long time since you have had a real meal," said my sister-in-law. How true it was! But I felt constrained, and ate very little. Here were the people and the things I had so longed to be with; but I caught myself regarding them with the eyes of a Western American. Suddenly—at one glance, as it were—I grasped the answer to the problem that had puzzled me so long; for here in the persons of those dear to me I was seeing myself as those others had seen me.

I went about revisiting old scenes and found that everything had changed in my brief absence. My friends were not the same; the East Side was not the same. They never would be the same. What had come over them? My kinsfolk and my old companions looked me over and declared that it was I who had become transformed. I had become soberer. I carried myself differently. There was an unfamiliar reserve, something mingled of coldness and melancholy, in my eye. My very speech had a new intonation. It was more incisive, but less fluent, less cordial, they thought. Perhaps so. At any rate, while my people were still dear to me, and always would be dear to me, the atmosphere about them repelled me. If it was I who had changed, then, as I took in the little world I had emerged from, I could not help telling myself that the change was a salutary one.

While calling at the old basement bookshop on East Broadway I suddenly heard a horrible wailing and lamenting on the street. A funeral procession was hurrying by, followed by several women in an open carriage. Their hair was flying, their faces were red with weeping, their bodies were swaying grotesquely to the rhythm of their violent cries. The oldest in the group continued mechanically to address the body in the hearse: "Husband dear, upon whom have you left us? Upon whom, husband dear?" A young girl facing her in the vehicle looked about in a terrified manner, seized every now and then the hand of her afflicted mother, and tried to quiet her. The frightful scene, with its tragic display, its abysmal ludicrousness, its barbarous noise, revolted me. I had seen the like of it before, but that was in another life. I had once been part of such a performance myself, and the grief of it still lingered somewhere in my motley soul. But now I could only think of the affecting simplicity, the quiet, unobtrusive solemnity of a burial I had witnessed the previous spring in the West.

The afternoon following my arrival I flew up-town to see Esther. She waved to me and smiled as I approached—she had been waiting on the "stoop." As she shook my hand in her somewhat masculine fashion she took me in with a glance, and the first thing she said was, "What a genteel person you have become! You have changed astonishingly." "Do you think so?" I asked her. "I am afraid I haven't. At least they do not think so in Missouri." Then she told me that she had got only ten points, but that she was expecting three more in the fall. She was almost resigned to wait another year before entering college. That would enable her to make her total requirements, save up a little more money, and get her breath.... "But let us not talk about my troubles. You are full of things to tell me, I know."

Yes, I had lots I wanted to say, but I did not know where to begin; and the one thing that was uppermost in my mind I was afraid to utter lest she should misunderstand and feel injured and reproach me. I did not want her to reproach me on first meeting. I wanted to give myself time as well as her. And so we fell into one of those customary long silences, and for a while I felt at home again, and reflected that perhaps I had been hasty in letting the first poignant reactions mislead me....

[They then attend a political gathering downtown, where the featured speaker attacked American capitalism to a crowd composed largely of poor immigrants. Ravage finds the speaker to be "honest and fiery and ill-informed," and after he and Esther leave the hall he decides to declare "what I had hesitated to tell her earlier in the evening."]

"Save yourself, my dear friend. Run as fast as you can. You will find a bigger and a freer world than this. Promise me that you will follow me to the West this fall. You will thank me for it. Those big, genuine people out in Missouri are the salt of the earth. Whatever they may think about the problem of universal brotherhood, they have already solved it for their next-door neighbors. There is no need of the social revolution in Missouri; they have a generous slice of the kingdom of heaven."

Maybe I was exaggerating, but that was how I felt. From this distance and from these surroundings Missouri and the new world she meant to me was enchanting and heroic. The loneliness I had endured, the snubbing, the ridicule, the inner struggles—all the dreariness and the sadness of my life in exile—had faded out of the picture, and what remained was only an idealized vision of the clean manhood, the large human dignity, the wholesome, bracing atmosphere of it, which contrasted so strikingly with the things around me.

No, there was no sense in deceiving myself, the East Side had somehow ceased to be my world. I had thought a few days ago that I was going home. I had yelled to Harvey [a college friend] from the train as it was pulling out of the station at Columbia, "I am going home, old man!" But I had merely come to another strange land. In the fall I would return to that other exile. I was, indeed, a man without a country.

During that entire summer, while I opened gates on an Elevated train in Brooklyn, I tussled with my problem. It was quite apparent to me from the first what its solution must be. I knew that now there was no going back for me; that my only hope lay in continuing in the direction I had taken, however painful it may be to my loved ones and to myself. But for a long time I could not admit it to myself. A host of voices and sights and memories had awakened within me that clutched me to my people and to my past. As long as I remained in New York I kept up the tragic farce of making Sunday calls on brother Harry and pretending that all was as before, that America and education had changed nothing, that I was still one of them. I had taken a room in a remote quarter of Brooklyn, where there were few immigrants, under the pretense that it was nearer to the railway barns. But I was deceiving no one but myself. Most of my relatives, who had received me so heartily when I arrived, seemed to be avoiding Harry's house on Sundays, and on those rare occasions when I ran into one of them he seemed frigid and ill-at-ease. Once Paul said to me: "You are very funny. It looks as if you were ashamed of the family. You aren't really, are you? You know they said you would be when you went away. There is a lot of foolish talk about it. Everybody speaks of Harry and me as the doctor's brothers. Can't you warm up?"

I poured out my heart in a letter to Harvey. If a year ago I had been told that I would be laying my sorrows and my disappointments in my own kindred before any one out there, I would have laughed at the idea. But that barbarian in Missouri was the only human being, strangely enough, in whom I could now confide with any hope of being understood. I tried to convey to him some idea of the agonizing moral experience I was going through. I told him that I was aching to get back to Columbia (how apt the name was!) to take up again where I had left off the process of my transformation, and to get through with it as soon as might be.

And in the fall I went back—this time a week before college opened—and was met by Harvey at the station, just as those rural-looking boys had been met by their friends the year before. When I reached the campus I was surprised to see how many people knew me. Scores of them came up and slapped me on the back and shook hands in their hearty, boisterous fashion, and hoped that I had had a jolly summer. I was asked to join boarding-clubs, to become a member in debating societies, to come and see this fellow or that in his room. It took me off my feet, this sudden geniality of my fellows toward me. I had not been aware how, throughout the previous year, the barriers between us had been gradually and steadily breaking down. It came upon me all at once. I felt my heart going out to my new friends. I had become one of them. I was not a man without a country. I was an American.

Source: Ravage, M.E. *An American in the Making: The Life Story of an Immigrant.* New York: Harper, 1917, pp. Vii-viii, 59-61, 137-38, 258-66.

Coolidge Signs the Immigration Act of 1924

On May 26, 1924, President Calvin Coolidge signed the Immigration Act of 1924 into law. This bill dramatically curtailed immigration into the United States, and it remained the major immigration law of the land for the next four decades.

Coolidge himself had mixed feelings about the legislation. After signing the bill, he declared his satisfaction with the bill's National Origins Quota provisions, which dramatically reduced overall immigration to the United States. But he condemned language in the bill that ended almost all emigration from Japan and other parts of eastern Asia. Noting that Japan's government had already implemented steps to discourage Japanese workers from emigrating, he argued that the bill was needlessly insulting. He also made sure to note that the bill still permitted some Asian tourists, students, and professional people to enter the United States, and that it did not call for the deportation of Japanese and other Asians already in America.

Coolidge's emphasis on these few bright spots reflected his concern about the law's potential impact on U.S.-Japan relations. Still, Coolidge's objections to the explicitly anti-Asian provisions contained in the Act were not strong enough to keep him from signing the overall bill into law. Following is the complete text of his signing statement.

In signing this Bill, which in its main features I heartily approve, I regret the impossibility of severing from it the exclusion provision which, in the light of existing law, affects especially the Japanese. I gladly recognize that the enactment of this provision does not imply any change in our sentiment of admiration and cordial friendship for the Japanese people, a sentiment which has had and will continue to have abundant manifestation. The Bill rather expresses the determination of the Congress to exercise its prerogative in defining by legislation the control of immigration instead of leaving it to international arrangements. It should be noted the Bill exempts from the exclusion provision government officials, those coming to this country as tourists or temporarily for business or pleasure, those in transit, seamen, those already resident here and returning from temporary absences, professors, ministers of religion, students, and those who enter solely to carry on trade in pursuance of existing treaty provisions.

But we have had for many years an understanding with Japan by which the Japanese Government has voluntarily undertaken to prevent the emigration of laborers to the United States, and in view of this historic relation and of the feeling which inspired it, it would have been much better in my judgment, and more effective in the actual control of immigration, if we had continued to invite the cooperation which Japan was ready to give and had thus avoided creating any ground for misapprehension by an unnecessary statutory enactment. That course would not have derogated from the authority of the Congress to deal with the question in any exigency requiring its action. There is scarcely any ground for disagreement as to the result we want, but this method of securing it is unnecessary and deplorable at this time. If the exclusion provision stood alone I should disapprove it without hesitation, if sought in this way at this time. But this Bill is a comprehensive measure dealing with the whole subject of immigration and setting up the necessary administrative machinery. The present Quota Act, of 1921, will terminate on June 30th next. It is of great importance that a comprehensive measure should take its place, and that the arrangements for its administration should be provided at once in order to avoid hardship and confusion. I must therefore consider the Bill as a whole, and the imperative need of the country for legislation of this general character. For this reason the Bill is approved.

Source: Coolidge, Calvin. "Statement Issued to the Press by President Coolidge," May 26, 1924, quoted in John Bond Trevor, *An Analysis of the American Immigration Act of 1924*. New York: Carnegie Endowment for International Peace, Division of Intercourse and Education, 1924, pp. 75-6.

A Criticism of "Guest Worker" Proposals

During the opening years of the twenty-first century, the United States became mired in an emotional debate about the problem of illegal immigration. Much of the argument has focused on how America should handle the millions of illegal immigrants—most of them from Mexico and other parts of Latin America—already working in the United States. Some people believe that the United States should re-classify these illegal immigrants as "guest workers" who would be eligible for eventual citizenship, provided they passed criminal background checks, learned English, obtained steady work, and met other criteria. But critics claim that "guest worker" proposals and other pro-immigration measures unfairly reward illegal aliens for breaking U.S. laws. Many opponents also believe that too much immigration—legal or illegal—hurts the American economy and society.

In the following Washington Post *column by Robert J. Samuelson, a nationally known writer on economic issues, the author argues that "guest worker" proposals are deeply flawed. In this piece, Samuelson refers to two specific immigration proposals of the mid-2000s—one by President George W. Bush and one jointly proposed by Democratic Senator Ted Kennedy and Republican Senator John McCain. Neither of these proposals received enough Congressional support for passage.*

Economist Philip Martin of the University of California likes to tell a story about the state's tomato industry. In the early 1960s, growers relied on seasonal Mexican laborers, brought in under the government's "bracero" program. The Mexicans picked the tomatoes that were then processed into ketchup and other products. In 1964 Congress killed the program despite growers' warnings that its abolition would doom their industry. What happened? Well, plant scientists developed oblong tomatoes that could be harvested by machine. Since then, California's tomato output has risen fivefold.

It's a story worth remembering, because we're being warned again that we need huge numbers of "guest workers"—meaning unskilled laborers from Mexico and Central America—to relieve U.S. "labor shortages." Indeed, the shortages will supposedly worsen as baby boomers retire. President Bush wants an open-ended program. Sens. Edward M. Kennedy (D-Mass.) and John McCain (R-Ariz.) advocate initially admitting 400,000 guest workers annually. The Senate is considering these and other plans.

Gosh, they're all bad ideas.

Guest workers would mainly legalize today's vast inflows of illegal immigrants, with the same consequence: We'd be importing poverty. This isn't because these immigrants aren't hardworking; many are. Nor is it because they don't assimilate; many do. But they generally don't go home, assimilation is slow and the ranks of the poor are constantly replenished. Since 1980 the number of Hispanics with incomes below the government's poverty line (about $19,300 in 2004 for a family of four) has risen 162 percent. Over the same period, the number of non-Hispanic whites in poverty rose 3 percent and the number of blacks, 9.5 percent. What we have now—and would with guest workers—is a conscious policy of creating poverty in the United States while relieving it in Mexico. By and large, this is a bad bargain for the United States. It stresses local schools, hospitals and housing; it feeds social tensions (witness the Minutemen). To be sure, some Americans get cheap housecleaning or landscaping services. But if more mowed their own lawns or did their own laundry, it wouldn't be a tragedy.

The most lunatic notion is that admitting more poor Latino workers would ease the labor market strains of retiring baby boomers. The two aren't close substitutes for each other. Among immigrant Mexican and Central American workers in 2004, only 7 percent had a college degree and nearly 60 percent lacked a high school diploma, according to the Congressional Budget Office. Among native-born U.S. workers, 32 percent had a college degree and only 6 percent did not have a high school diploma. Far from softening the social problems of an aging society, more poor immigrants might aggravate them by pitting older retirees against younger Hispanics for limited government benefits.

It's a myth that the U.S. economy "needs" more poor immigrants. The illegal immigrants already here represent only about 4.9 percent of the labor force, the Pew Hispanic Center reports. In no major occupation are they a majority. They're 36 percent of insulation workers, 28 percent of drywall installers and 20 percent of cooks. They're drawn here by wage differences, not labor "shortages." In 2004, the median hourly wage in Mexico was $1.86, compared with $9 for Mexicans working in the United States, said Rakesh Kochhar of Pew. With high labor turnover in the jobs they take, most new illegal immigrants can get work by accepting wages slightly below prevailing levels.

Hardly anyone thinks that most illegal immigrants will leave. But what would happen if new illegal immigration stopped and wasn't replaced by guest workers? Well, some employers would raise wages to attract U.S. workers. Facing greater labor costs, some industries would—like the tomato growers in the 1960s—find ways to minimize those costs. As to the rest, what's wrong with higher wages for the poorest workers? From 1994 to 2004, the wages of high school dropouts rose only 2.3 percent (after inflation) compared with 11.9 percent for college graduates.

President Bush says his guest worker program would "match willing foreign workers with willing American employers, when no Americans can be found to fill the jobs." But at some higher wage, there would be willing Americans. The number of native high school dropouts with jobs declined by 1.3 million from 2000 to 2005, estimates Steven Camarota of the Center for Immigration Studies, which favors less immigration. Some lost jobs to immigrants. Unemployment remains high for some groups (9.3 percent for African Americans, 12.7 percent for white teenagers).

Business organizations understandably support guest worker programs. They like cheap labor and ignore the social consequences. What's more perplexing is why liberals, staunch opponents of poverty and inequality, support a program that worsens poverty and inequality. Poor immigrant workers hurt the wages of unskilled Americans. The only question is how much. Studies suggest a range "from negligible to an earnings reduction of almost 10 percent," according to the CBO.

It's said that having guest workers is better than having poor illegal immigrants. With legal status, they'd have rights and protections. They'd have more peace of mind and face less exploitation by employers. This would be convincing if its premise were incontestable: that we can't control our southern border. But that's unproved. We've never tried a policy of real barriers and strict enforcement against companies that hire illegal immigrants. Until that's shown to be ineffective, we shouldn't adopt guest worker programs that don't solve serious social problems—but add to them.

Source: Samuelson, Robert J. "We Don't Need 'Guest Workers,'" *Washington Post,* March 22, 2006, p. A21.

A Proposal to Increase Legal Immigration

In the following column, writer Michael Kinsley challenges Americans who view illegal immigration as one of the nation's biggest problems. He notes that many opponents of illegal immigration say that their views are based on respect for the sanctity of American laws—which illegal immigrants break by entering the United States without government approval. But Kinsley questions whether opponents might actually be using this argument to mask their wider opposition to immigration in any form.

What you are supposed to say about immigration—what most of the presidential candidates say, what the radio talk jocks say—is that you are not against immigration. Not at all. You salute the hard work and noble aspirations of those who are lining up at American consulates around the world. But that is legal immigration. What you oppose is illegal immigration.

This formula is not very helpful. We all oppose breaking the law, or we ought to. Saying that you oppose illegal immigration is like saying you oppose illegal drug use or illegal speeding. Of course you do, or should. The question is whether you think the law draws the line in the right place. Should using marijuana be illegal? Should the speed limit be raised—or lowered? The fact that you believe in obeying the law reveals nothing about what you think the law ought to be, or why.

Another question: Why are you so upset about this particular form of lawbreaking? After all, there are lots of laws, not all of them enforced with vigor. The suspicion naturally arises that the illegality is not what bothers you. What bothers you is the immigration. There is an easy way to test this. Reducing illegal immigration is hard, but increasing legal immigration would be easy. If your view is that legal immigration is good and illegal immigration is bad, how about increasing legal immigration? How about doubling it? Any takers? So in the end, this is not really a debate about illegal immigration. This is a debate about immigration.

And it's barely a debate at all. On the Democratic side, the arcane issue of whether illegals should be able to get a driver's license has bitten both Hillary Clinton and Barack Obama. On the Republican side, the candidates take turns accusing one another of committing some act of human decency toward illegals, and indignantly denying that they did any such thing. Immigration has long divided both parties, with advocates and opponents in each. Among Republicans, support for immigration was economic (corporations), while opposition was cultural (nativists). Among Democrats, it was the reverse: support for immigration was cultural (ethnic groups), while opposition was economic (unions). Now, for whatever reason, support for immigration is limited to an eccentric alliance of high-minded Council on Foreign Relations types, the mainstream media, high-tech entrepreneurs, Latinos, the *Wall Street Journal* editorial page and President George W. Bush. Everyone else, it seems, is agin [against].

Maybe the aginners are right, and immigration is now damaging our country, stealing jobs and opportunity, ripping off taxpayers, fragmenting our culture. I doubt it, but maybe so. Certainly, it's true that we can't let in everyone who wants to come. There is some number of immigrants that is too many. I don't believe we're past that point, but maybe we are. In any event, a democracy has the right to decide that it has reached such a point. There is no obligation to be fair to foreigners.

But let's not kid ourselves that all we care about is obeying the law and all we are asking illegals to do is go home and get in line like everybody else. We know perfectly well that the line is too long, and we are basically telling people to go home and not come back.

Let's not kid ourselves, either, about who we are telling this to. To characterize illegal immigrants as queue-jumping, lawbreaking scum is seriously unjust. The motives of illegal immigrants—which can be summarized as "a better life"—are identical to those of legal immigrants. In fact, they are largely identical to the motives of our own parents, grandparents and great-grandparents when they immigrated. And not just that. Ask yourself, of these three groups—today's legal and illegal immigrants and the immigrants of generations ago—which one has proven most dramatically its appreciation of our country? Which one has shown the most gumption, the most willingness to risk all to get to the U.S. and the most willingness to work hard once here? Well, everyone's story is unique. But who loves the U.S. most? On average, probably, the winners of this American-values contest would be the illegals, doing our dirty work under constant fear of eviction, getting thrown out and returning again and again.

And how about those of us lucky enough to have been born here? How would we do against the typical illegal alien in a "prove how much you love America" reality TV show?

Source: Kinsley, Michael. "Kidding Ourselves about Immigration," *Time*, Dec. 06, 2007.

"A Yearning That Is Timeless"

In the following brief article, National Catholic Reporter *contributor Thomas W. Roberts makes the case that today's illegal aliens from Mexico and other countries are motivated to come to America by the same hopes and dreams that drove his own Italian ancestors to make their way to the United States a century earlier.*

There is a story my grandfather was fond of telling, in his halting English, to whoever would listen. It was about the day he went to his mother as a young man, presumably somewhere near a tiny house on a hillside overlooking the Adriatic on Italy's East Coast, to tell her he was leaving.

"I tol'a my mom I go to 'merica," he'd say, chopping off the first "A" and roiling the "r".

"And in-a two days," he said, brushing his hands together to show he'd made quick work of it, "I'm-a gone."

He stowed away in a ship, probably in one that sailed from Naples, on the opposite coast from the small home that, as of a few years ago when I saw it, was still hanging precariously and in dilapidated shape from that hillside.

I think of that story often in this time of debate over a new wave of immigrants. I don't know if my grandfather consulted the laws at that time. I don't think so, nor do I think he had any idea what he would face in America. He knew over here was better, he knew how to work hard. He went for it.

He was one of dozens of Rabottinis (turned Roberts), Palladinos, Morellos, Mammarellas, DelMutos, Gambinos, and others who found their way to Southeastern Pennsylvania at the turn of the last century and settled. They talked funny—and some never became proficient at speaking English. They managed. Others took their Italian into grammar school and eventually managed to catch up with and surpass others in their classes. They farmed. They grew into entrepreneurs from the bottom of the heap, they built businesses, they eventually taught in high schools and universities, they became all manner of workers, white collar, blue collar and every shade in between. They helped build lodges and service clubs and churches and town halls. They sent money home and they sent passage for others in their families. They acted as agents for new arrivals, setting them up in jobs with their own employers.

They were the Mexicans of the turn of the century, and they did whatever they needed to do to get here. From 1890 until about 1920 some 4 million Italians—nearly a quarter of all immigrants to the United States—sought a new start here, most fleeing poverty and seeking economic advantage.

Of course the comparison fails on a number of counts. At the turn of the century, there were only 10 million foreign-born in the United States and there were fewer laws regarding immigration. Today, the influx of immigrants is far more regulated, except, of course, along the southern border, where neither fences, border guards nor the threat of death in the desert has stopped the flow of immigrants.

The problem is complex. Some of those complexities have been dealt with at length in past stories and, in today's issue, on the back page. The comparison, however, holds up in the yearning that is timeless—to escape poverty, to have a better life, to assure that life will be better for one's children. It is at the heart of the entrepreneurial spirit that we so admire in other circumstances. Globalization makes borders porous for all sorts of goods and ideas and services. It will take more than jingoistic language about security to fashion a reasonable plan to make that border less porous to people and to do justice to those who have been a part of this culture for a long time.

Source: Roberts, Thomas W. "A Yearning That Is Timeless," *National Catholic Reporter,* April 7, 2006, p. 2.

IMPORTANT PEOPLE, PLACES, AND TERMS

Addams, Jane (1860-1935)
Social worker and activist for immigrants and poor Americans

Assimilation
The process in which an immigrant becomes part of another culture, usually by adopting the language, customs, and other characteristics of that culture

Contract laborer
Immigrant worker who makes arrangements to take a specific job before making the journey to America

Coolidge, Calvin (1872-1933)
30th president of the United States, who served from 1923 to 1929

Dillingham Commission
A joint Congressional committee that issued a series of reports in 1910-11 identifying immigrants as a major source of America's social and economic problems—and urging the institution of a literacy test for all immigrants

Emigration
The act of leaving one country or region for another with the intention of establishing a new life

Group settlement
Instances in which large groups of families from single communities immigrate to America together

Hall, Prescott F. (1868-1921)
Co-Founder and General Secretary of the Immigration Restriction League

Hoar, George Frisbie (1826-1904)
Republican Senator from Massachusetts who was a long-time advocate for immigrants

Immigration
The act of entering a country or region for the purpose of establishing a new life

Immigration Restriction League
Leading anti-immigration organization of the late nineteenth and early twentieth centuries

Know-Nothings
American political party that experienced a brief run of popularity in the 1850s as a result of its strong anti-immigration stance

Lodge, Henry Cabot (1850-1924)
Republican Senator and anti-immigration legislator from Massachusetts

Melting Pot
A place where people—often immigrants—from different cultures and ethnic and racial backgrounds blend together to form an integrated society

Migration chains
Mass emigration from Europe in which one or two individuals from a family or community establish themselves in America, then signal for others to follow

Nativists
Native-born Americans who believe that they and others born in the United States deserve special protection and consideration in U.S. law and business, especially in comparison to immigrants

Naturalized citizens
People who obtain U.S. citizenship after emigrating from a foreign land and meeting federal citizenship requirements

New World
North America

Old World
Europe

Powderly, Terence V. (1849-1924)
Labor Union Leader and U.S. Commissioner of Immigration, 1897-1902

Settlement Houses
Neighborhood centers established by reformers to help immigrants and other residents of urban slums

Steerage
The notoriously filthy and crowded section of ships that was set aside for poor passengers immigrating to America in the nineteenth and early twentieth centuries

Tenements
Crowded apartment buildings that became common in urban slums in the nineteenth century

Trachoma
Highly contagious disease of the eye

Watchorn, Robert (1859?-1944)
Commissioner of Immigration at Ellis Island, 1905-1909

Williams, William (1862-1947)
Commissioner of Immigration at Ellis Island, 1902-05, 1909-13

Xenophobia
Strong fear or hatred of strangers or foreigners

CHRONOLOGY

1607

English settlers land in what is today Chesapeake Bay, Virginia, and establish the colony of Jamestown.

1619

The first African slaves are transported to North America.

1625

A settlement called New Amsterdam—modern-day New York—is founded by the Dutch.

1776

The thirteen colonies of the United States of America declare their independence from England.

1781

The Revolutionary War ends with an American victory, and two years later England signs the Treaty of Paris formally recognizing the legitimacy of the United States.

1790

The United States passes its first naturalization law, which states that free white men who live in the country for at least two years are eligible for citizenship.

1791

The United States approves ten amendments to the U.S. Constitution collectively known as the Bill of Rights.

1798

Congress passes the Alien and Sedition Acts, which give federal authorities new powers to deport "undesirable" aliens.

1845

The Great Potato Famine strikes in Ireland, ushering in years of misery and starvation for the Irish people—and convincing many to leave for America.

1848

The United States expands its territory to include modern-day Texas, California, and a broad swath of the American Southwest after winning the Mexican-American War.

1855

Castle Garden, the first immigration station in the United States, opens its doors in New York City.

1865

The American Civil War comes to an end.

1868

The United States adopts the Fourteenth Amendment, which grants citizenship to the nation's African-American population.

1869

America's first transcontinental railroad is completed with the help of thousands of Chinese laborers.

1881

Russian Czar Alexander II is assassinated. After Jews are falsely blamed for plotting his death, anti-Jewish riots break out in Russia and many Jewish families decide to leave for America.

1882

The Chinese Exclusion Act becomes law.

1885

Congress passes a law against "contract laborers"—immigrants who come to America with firm employment already lined up in advance.

1886

The Statue of Liberty is formally dedicated in New York City.

1890

Jane Addams establishes the Hull House settlement house in Chicago.

1891

The Immigration Act of 1891 requires all aliens entering the United States to pass examinations.

1892

The federal immigration station on Ellis Island in New York City opens its doors.

1897

Fire destroys many of the original buildings at Ellis Island, forcing authorities to rebuild the facilities.

A bill requiring all immigrants to pass a literacy test passes in both houses of Congress but is vetoed by President Grover Cleveland.

1910-11

A joint Congressional committee called the Dillingham Commission issues a series of reports blaming America's problems on immigrants and calling for a literacy test for all prospective immigrants.

1913

Congress passes another literacy test bill, but it is vetoed by President Howard Taft.

1914

World War I begins in Europe.

1915

President Woodrow Wilson vetoes yet another Congressional bill calling for a literacy test for immigrants wishing to enter the United States.

1917

Congress overrides a 1916 veto by President Wilson and votes the Federal Immigration Act—which imposes a literacy test for immigrants—into law.

United States enters World War I.

1918

World War I ends with victory for the United States and its allies against Germany and the other so-called Central Powers.

A horrible flu epidemic sweeps across the world, claiming as many as 40 million lives before it runs its course in mid-1919.

1920

Women receive the right to vote after ratification of the Nineteenth Amendment.

1924

The Immigration Act of 1924 is signed into law, dramatically reducing legal immigration into the United States.

1943

The Chinese Exclusion Act is repealed.

1948

The Displaced Persons Act admits 400,000 refugees from war-torn Europe.

1952

The McCarran-Walter Act becomes law and changes the U.S. quota system for immigrants.

1954

Federal officials close the Ellis Island immigration station.

1965

President Lyndon B. Johnson signs the Immigration and Naturalization Act, which scraps the old immigration quota system and replaces it with a whole new system.

1986

The renovated Statue of Liberty is unveiled in a three-day July 4 weekend celebration.

President Ronald Reagan signs the Immigration Reform and Control Act into law.

1990

Ellis Island is re-opened as a museum dedicated to preserving the history of American immigration.

SOURCES FOR FURTHER STUDY

Chermayeff, Ivan, Fred Wasserman, and Mary J. Shapiro. *Ellis Island: An Illustrated History of the Immigrant Experience.* New York: Macmillan, 1991. This lavishly illustrated volume provides a good overview of the experiences of European and other immigrants during the years when Ellis Island served as the gateway to America. It also covers the abandonment and subsequent restoration of Ellis Island.

Ellis Island National Monument. Available online at http://www.nps.gov/elis. This is the National Park Service website for Ellis Island. It contains a wide range of historical information on the facility, as well as special links for teachers and students.

Handlin, Oscar. *The Uprooted: The Epic Story of the Great Migrations that Made the American People.* 1952. Reprint. Philadelphia: University of Pennsylvania Press, 2002. One of the best books ever published on the immigration experience. Instead of engaging in long discussions of immigration policy or national economics, the author focuses on the daily experiences and emotions of ordinary immigrants during their voyage to America and after their passage through the gates of Ellis Island.

Immigration: The Living Mosaic of People, Culture, and Hope. Available online at http://library.thinkquest.org/20619. An interesting website that breaks much of its historical coverage down by individual ethnic and religious groups.

Immigration to the United States, 1789-1930. Harvard Open Collections Program. Available online at http://ocp.hul.harvard.edu/immigration. This remarkable, easy-to-use online collection features immigration documents and other materials from the libraries, museums, and archives of Harvard University.

Yans-McLaughlin, Virginia, and Marjorie Lightman. *Ellis Island and the Peopling of America: The Official Guide.* New York: New Press, 1997. This historical overview was published by the Ellis Island-Statue of Liberty Foundation. It includes historic photographs, interesting excerpts from official reports and other primary documents, and a good overview of Ellis Island history.

BIBLIOGRAPHY

Books and Periodicals

Allen, Frederick Lewis. *Only Yesterday: An Informal History of the 1920s*. New York: Harper & Brothers, 1931.

Bowden, Charles. "Exodus," *Orion Magazine*, July-August 2008.

Brownstone, David M., Irene M. Franck, and Douglass Brownstone. *Island of Hope, Island of Tears*. New York: MetroBooks, 2003.

Chermayeff, Ivan, Fred Wasserman, and Mary J. Shapiro. *Ellis Island: An Illustrated History of the Immigrant Experience*. New York: Macmillan, 1991.

Daniels, Roger. *Guarding the Golden Door: American Immigration Policy and Immigrants Since 1882*. New York: Hill and Wang, 2004.

Dubofsky, Melvyn. *Industrialism and the American Worker, 1865-1920*. Arlington Heights, IL: Harlan Davidson, 1985.

Guzda, Henry P. "Ellis Island a Welcome Site? Only after Years of Reform." *Monthly Labor Review*, July 1986.

Hagen, Charles, Norman Kotker, and Robert Twombly. *Ellis Island: Echoes from a Nation's Past*. New York: Aperture, 2005.

Handlin, Oscar. *The Uprooted: The Epic Story of the Great Migrations that Made the American People*. 1952. Reprint. Philadelphia: University of Pennsylvania Press, 2002.

Immigrants: The New Americans. Editors of Time-Life Books. New York: Time-Life, 1999.

Jacoby, Tamar. *Reinventing the Melting Pot: The New Immigrants and What It Means to be an American*. New York: Basic Books, 2004.

Krikorian, Mark. *The New Case against Immigration: Both Legal and Illegal*. New York: Sentinel HC, 2008.

McBee, Randy D. *Dance Hall Days: Intimacy and Leisure Among Working-Class Immigrants in the United States*. New York: New York University Press, 2000.

McGerr, Michael. *A Fierce Discontent: The Rise and Fall of the Progressive Movement in America*. New York: Oxford University Press, 2003.

Meltzer, Milton. *Bound for America: The Story of the European Immigrants*. New York: Benchmark, 2001.

Riley, Jason L. *Let Them In: The Case for Open Borders*. New York: Gotham, 2008.

Sorin, Gerald. *The Jewish People in America. Vol. III: A Time for Building, The Third Migration, 1880-1920*. Baltimore: Johns Hopkins University Press, 1992.

Tichenor, Daniel J. *Dividing Lines: The Politics of Immigration Control in America*. Princeton, NJ: Princeton University Press, 2002.

Vedder, Richard, Lowell Gallaway, and Stephen Moore. "The Immigration Problem: Then and Now." *The Independent Review*, vol. 4, no. 3, Winter 2000.

Yans-McLaughlin, Virginia, and Marjorie Lightman. *Ellis Island and the Peopling of America: The Official Guide*. New York: New Press, 1997.

Internet

Cannato, Vincent. "Coming to America: Ellis Island and New York City." *History Now: American History Online,* March 2007. Available online at www.historynow.org/03_2007/historian2.html.

Immigration: The Living Mosaic of People, Culture, and Hope. Available online at http://library.thinkquest.org/20619.

Immigration to the United States, 1789-1930. Harvard Open Collections Program. Available online at http://ocp.hul.harvard.edu/immigration.

DVDs

Dying to Get In. DVD. Mooncusser Films, 2007.

Ellis Island. DVD. History Channel, 2003.

Out of Ireland: The Story of Irish Emigration to America. DVD. Shanachie, 1997.

PHOTO AND ILLUSTRATION CREDITS

Chapter Six: Lithograph by J. Keppler, Prints and Photographs Division, Library of Congress, LC-USZC2-1242 (p. 84); Frances Benjamin Johnston Collection, Prints and Photographs Division, Library of Congress, LC-USZ62-68226 (p. 86); Reproduction of cartoon drawing by Raymond O. Evans, Prints and Photographs Division, Library of Congress, LC-USZ62-52584 (p. 88); National Photo Company Collection, Prints and Photographs Division, Library of Congress, LC-USZ62-96154 (p. 92).

Chapter Seven: Hulton Archive/Getty Images (p. 96); Photo by Jet Lowe, Historic American Engineering Record, Prints and Photographs Division, Library of Congress, HAER NY, 31-NEYO, 89-24 (p. 99); Courtesy, Ronald Reagan Presidential Library (p. 103); David McNew/Online USA/Getty Images (p. 105); Jeff Topping/Reuters/Landov (p. 107); Lucas Jackson/Reuters/Landov (p. 110).

Biographies: Prints and Photographs Division, Library of Congress, LC-USZ62-10598 (p. 117); Brady-Handy Photograph Collection, Prints and Photographs Division, Library of Congress, LC-DIG-cwpbh-03673 (p. 124); Photo by Pirie MacDonald, Prints and Photographs Division, Library of Congress, LC-USZ62-36185 (p. 127); Ohio Historical Society (p. 132); Brown Brothers, Sterling, PA 18463 (p. 135).

INDEX

Watchorn, Robert, 56, 57, 59, 135 (ill.), 140
    biography, 135-37
Weber, John B., 56
Welfare Reform Act. *See* Personal
    Responsibility and Work Opportunity
    Reconciliation Act
Wells, H.G., 4-5
Welsh immigrants, 9-10

Williams, George Henry, 83
Williams, William, 56-57, 59, 85, 136
    biography, 138-41
Wilson, Woodrow, 90, 91, 123, 129, 130
Windom, William, 45-46
With Poor Immigrants in America (Graham),
    162-71
Workingmen's Party, 145, 147